THE MURDERS OF TUPAC AND BIGGIE

BY SUE BRADFORD EDWARDS

CONTENT CONSULTANT

AARON X. SMITH
PROFESSOR OF AFRICAN AMERICAN STUDIES
TEMPLE UNIVERSITY

AMERICAN
CRIME
STORIES

Essential Library

An Imprint of Abdo Publishing | abdobooks.com

ABDOBOOKS.COM

Published by Abdo Publishing, a division of ABDO, PO Box 398166, Minneapolis, Minnesota 55439. Copyright © 2020 by Abdo Consulting Group, Inc. International copyrights reserved in all countries. No part of this book may be reproduced in any form without written permission from the publisher. Essential Library™ is a trademark and logo of Abdo Publishing.

Printed in the United States of America, North Mankato, Minnesota.
102019
012020

Cover Photos: RTNBunn/MediaPunch/IPX/AP Images (right); Pat Johnson/MediaPunch/IPX/AP Images (left)
Interior Photos: Jeff Kravitz/FilmMagic/Getty Images, 4–5; Jim Laurie/AP Images, 7; Lennox McLendon/AP Images, 8; iStockphoto, 11; MTV Networks/Amaru Entertainment/PictureLux/The Hollywood Archive/Alamy, 13; AP Images, 17; Clarence Gatson/Gado/Archive Photos/Getty Images, 21; Pat Johnson/MediaPunch/IPX/AP Images, 22; Justin Sutcliffe/AP Images, 24; Raymond Boyd/Michael Ochs Archives/Getty Images, 27; Erik Pendzich/Rex Features, 32; Al Pereira/Michael Ochs Archives/Getty Images, 35, 45, 63; RGR Collection/Alamy, 36; Barry King/Alamy, 41; Shutterstock Images, 43, 87; Michele Eve/Splash News/Newscom, 48; Mark Lennihan/AP Images, 51; Red Line Editorial, 52; Philippe Psaila/Science Source, 55; Jim Ruymen/UPI/Newscom, 57; Frank Wiese/AP Images, 67; AdMedia/Splash News/Newscom, 70; Bei/Rex Features, 73; Ken Lubas/Los Angeles Times/Getty Images, 77; Paul Buck/EPA/AP Images, 80; Lynsey Addario/AP Images, 83; Perry van Munster/Alamy, 91; Lucas Jackson/Reuters/Newscom, 92; MediaPunch/Alamy, 96 (left); Startraks/Rex Features, 96 (right)

Editor: Charly Haley
Series Designer: Melissa Martin

LIBRARY OF CONGRESS CONTROL NUMBER: 2019942068
PUBLISHER'S CATALOGING-IN-PUBLICATION DATA

Names: Edwards, Sue Bradford, author.
Title: The murders of Tupac and Biggie / by Sue Bradford Edwards
Description: Minneapolis, Minnesota : Abdo Publishing, 2020 | Series: American crime stories | Includes online resources and index.
Identifiers: ISBN 9781532190124 (lib. bdg) | ISBN 9781532175978 (ebook)
Subjects: LCSH: Shakur, Tupac, 1971-1996 (Lesane Crooks)--Juvenile literature. | Notorious B.I.G., 1972-1997 (Christopher Wallace)--Juvenile literature. | Killing (Murder)--Juvenile literature. | Cold cases (Criminal investigation)--Juvenile literature. | Murder--Investigation--Juvenile literature. | Homicide--Juvenile literature.
Classification: DDC 364.152--dc23

CONTENTS

CHAPTER ONE

SHOT IN VEGAS

O n September 7, 1996, celebrity rapper Tupac Shakur was in Las Vegas to see boxer Mike Tyson fight Bruce Seldon at the MGM Grand hotel. Shakur's bodyguard, Frank Alexander, had arrived the day before. He knew that after the fight, Shakur and Suge Knight, cofounder of Death Row Records, planned to go to Knight's Club 662. One of the club rules was that no one could bring guns inside. This concerned Alexander, who was typically armed while working, because Shakur always attracted a crowd. The bodyguard worried about keeping his boss safe.

Tyson was a friend of Shakur's. As Tyson entered the boxing ring, Shakur's song "Let's Get It On" played from the speakers. Seldon was there to defend his heavyweight title. The crowd's energy was high. In just 109 seconds, Tyson had knocked Seldon down not once, but twice, and the fight was over.[1]

Tupac Shakur, *left*, and Suge Knight at the MGM Grand hotel and casino in Las Vegas

Shakur, Knight, and other members of their entourage were leaving the MGM Grand when an associate of Knight's started speaking to Shakur. Shakur hurried across the hotel lobby. When Alexander caught up, Shakur was in a fight with Orlando Anderson, a member of the South Side Crips gang. Soon, several members of the entourage were involved. Hotel security broke up the fight, and Shakur, Knight, and their group left to get ready for a night at Club 662.

The Shooting

Alexander planned to ride to Club 662 with Shakur in Knight's BMW, but Shakur handed the bodyguard a set of car keys. They were for a car that belonged to Kidada Jones, Shakur's girlfriend. Shakur wanted the bodyguard to drive the Outlawz, Shakur's band, to the club. Shakur would go in the BMW with Knight. Alexander agreed, and the group left the hotel.

Knight drove the BMW, and Shakur sat in the passenger seat. Music blasted, and the line of vehicles for Shakur's

TYSON AND TUPAC

In the early 1990s, Mike Tyson and Tupac Shakur met while they were waiting to get into an expensive club. Shakur was scheduled to perform, but the doorman didn't recognize him. Tyson didn't know why Shakur was there, but he remembered what it was like to be unknown and try to get into an exclusive club, so Tyson asked the doorman to let Shakur in. When Tyson eventually entered the club himself, Shakur was on the stage performing. The two became friends.

Mike Tyson, *left*, was popular among 1990s hip-hop artists and was often mentioned in lyrics. Hours before Shakur was killed, he watched Tyson win a boxing match.

entourage attracted attention. Shakur waved to fans on the sidewalk. Shortly after 11:00 p.m., the group stopped at a red light. A white Cadillac pulled up alongside Knight's vehicle, and someone in the Cadillac's back seat held a gun out the back window. This person fired fourteen shots into Knight's car.[2]

Knight stomped on the accelerator, made a U-turn, and drove down the street. Several other cars from the entourage followed. Knight came to a stop about a block later when one of his tires went flat.

Las Vegas police sergeant Chris Carroll, who was patrolling the area by bicycle, was the first officer at the scene of the

Knight's BMW was impounded by police as evidence after the shooting.

shooting. When he saw people jumping out of the vehicles, he pulled out his gun and ordered them to drop to the ground. Carroll saw that one man was still in the lead vehicle. He ordered the man out of the car but then saw that the man was hurt badly, shot four times. Carroll quickly learned that the injured man was Shakur.

"We have something called a dying declaration, where if someone is able to tell you, while they're dying and they believe they're going to die, who killed them, that's admissible in court," Carroll said to *E! News*. "It's not hearsay. So I asked him, 'What happened? Who shot you? Who did this?'"[3] Carroll did not get the name of the shooter before Shakur lost consciousness and was taken to the hospital.

At the Hospital

Knight had one wound to his head from a bullet fragment. Shakur was bleeding profusely from two bullets to his chest, one to his arm, and a fourth to his leg. At University Medical Center, he underwent emergency surgery. Doctors removed one of his lungs, which was seriously damaged and bleeding freely. Doctors told reporters that if Shakur survived, he would be able to get by with his one remaining lung.

Three days later, Shakur still had not regained consciousness. At this time, doctors told reporters that he had only a 20 percent chance of survival. Dr. John Fildes, chairman of the hospital's trauma center, spoke to the *New York Daily News* about chest wounds that were serious enough to require removing a lung. "Statistically, it carries a very high mortality rate," he said. "A patient may die from lack of oxygen or may bleed to death in the chest."[5]

Meanwhile, police questioned Knight about what he had witnessed at the scene of the shooting. Knight was close with Shakur, and he has been associated with the Mob Piru, a mainly African American street gang whose turf is on the east side of Compton, California. Knight sometimes hired members of the group to provide security for him. The group is affiliated with the Bloods, a large street gang in the Los Angeles area, and police believe Mob Piru's money comes from selling guns and drugs. The Bloods and Bloods-affiliated gangs are rivals of the Crips and their affiliates. Members of one group steal from or attack the other, as happened in the hotel lobby when Shakur attacked Anderson. Perhaps because of his gang ties or simply

CRIPS VS. BLOODS

The Crips gang formed in Los Angeles sometime between 1969 and 1971. It was initially known as the Cribs because members were so young, but it soon became the Crips. The Crips gang grew in size and power. This led to the formation of the Bloods gang as people sought safety from the Crips. The gangs fought over territory in Los Angeles throughout the 1970s and 1980s, developing a famously violent rivalry. In the 1980s, an increasing number of gangs across the country began to align themselves with either the Bloods or the Crips. A 1994 survey counted more than 1,100 gangs in 115 cities that included the words *Bloods* or *Crips* in their names.[6] Many street gangs today still align themselves with either gang. Bloods show their loyalty by wearing the color red, while Crips affiliates wear blue. The rivalry between the gangs has been portrayed in music and movies.

TUPAC'S LAST NIGHT

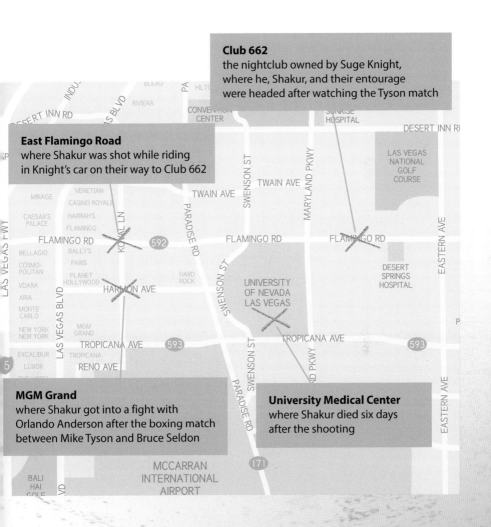

Club 662
the nightclub owned by Suge Knight, where he, Shakur, and their entourage were headed after watching the Tyson match

East Flamingo Road
where Shakur was shot while riding in Knight's car on their way to Club 662

MGM Grand
where Shakur got into a fight with Orlando Anderson after the boxing match between Mike Tyson and Bruce Seldon

University Medical Center
where Shakur died six days after the shooting

because he was an eyewitness, police believed Knight might know something that would help them find the killer, but he had nothing useful to tell the officers who questioned him.

The police were wary of another attack, so they placed guards at Shakur's hospital room. Jones, Shakur's girlfriend, and his mother, Afeni Shakur, were with him in the hospital. He was on life support in a medically induced coma, breathing only with the help of a machine. His body occasionally went into convulsions. His mother gave the doctors permission to remove her son from life support. On September 13, 1996, at 4:03 p.m., Tupac Shakur died.[7] He was cremated the following day.

Although the police investigated Shakur's murder, no one was ever arrested in connection with the shooting. Afeni was an outspoken critic of the investigation. In February 1997, she told

MEDICALLY INDUCED COMA

Patients who are in medically induced comas aren't asleep. They are unconscious because a doctor has given specific medications, such as propofol, pentobarbital, or thiopental, to induce the coma. Patients who are in comas must be monitored to make certain they maintain a regular heart rate, blood pressure, and breathing. Putting a patient into a coma is a serious step because it can have side effects. Patients are more likely to contract infections, especially chest infections, since they cannot cough to clear their lungs. Some patients who have come out of these comas report severe nightmares and hallucinations. Shakur was put into a coma because he kept trying to disconnect the machines that were keeping him alive and get out of bed.

Tupac Shakur, *right*, with his mother, Afeni, in an undated family photo

reporters, "Let me put it this way. When my son was lying in the hospital in a medically induced coma, the Las Vegas police went on national television telling everybody that he was not cooperating with their investigation. It was clear to me from Day 1 that the Las Vegas police never had any interest in solving the case of my son's murder."[8]

Las Vegas police sergeant Kevin Manning, who worked in the police department's metro homicide division, publicly defended the investigation. "We are as frustrated as anybody else that we have not been able to bring the individuals who shot Tupac Shakur to justice," Manning said. "We have suspects and we have bullets, but we still have no gun and no witnesses to identify the shooter."[9]

Gang-related killings are known for being difficult to solve. There is seldom much hard evidence, and witnesses are hesitant to talk. Manning said that detectives had taken thousands of phone tips and interviewed hundreds of witnesses in the Shakur case, following a variety of leads. "Tupac got the same treatment as any other homicide here," said Manning. "But you know what? We can't do it alone. We rely on cooperative citizens to step forward and help us solve crimes. And in Tupac's case, we got no cooperation whatsoever."[10] Many witnesses, including Shakur's associates, had arrest records that added to their unwillingness to interact with the police.

THE ASHES

Shakur was cremated, but not everyone agrees about what happened to his ashes. The Outlawz claimed they mixed a small amount into marijuana and smoked them. Some critics don't believe this statement because the band members can't agree when or where this happened. Shakur's mother scattered his ashes but told reporters more than one location where this took place. Most reporters wrote that she took them to Soweto, South Africa. Others were told that she spread some of them in a special location in Los Angeles, California, and the rest at her home garden in Stone Mountain, Georgia. Ashes can be easily divided, and it is possible that she spread some in each of these three locations.

Regardless of why the police did not get the information they needed, the case of Shakur's death remains unsolved. This may be part of the reason that people have developed so many theories about who murdered Shakur. Police blame the gangs, while some people believe that the police themselves or even the Federal Bureau of Investigation (FBI) may have had something to do with Shakur's death. Other people believe that money was the motive and that Shakur's own producer, Suge Knight, may have had Shakur killed before Shakur could sign with another record label. If not Knight, some people think maybe another producer, such as Sean Combs, had something to do with it. Still others believe that the culprit may have been former friend and fellow rapper Biggie Smalls.

CHAPTER TWO

TUPAC SHAKUR

From a young age, Tupac Shakur learned about inequality, social injustice, and the negative role that police and authority figures have often played in the lives of African Americans. His parents, Afeni Shakur and Billy Garland, were members of the Black Panthers. Also known as the Black Panther Party, this political group was founded in 1966 to oppose police violence against the African American community. Afeni Shakur's main role in the group was to raise bond money for members who had been arrested. But on April 2, 1969, she herself was arrested.

That morning, the Central Intelligence Agency (CIA), FBI, US Marshals Service, and New York State Police had coordinated raids on the homes of leading Black Panther members. They also raided the organization's community offices. These agencies arrested 21 Black Panthers, including Shakur, on suspicion of conspiring to start a race war. The Panther 21, as

A law enforcement officer escorts Afeni Shakur as she is arrested in 1969.

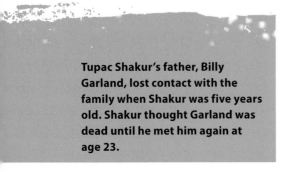

Tupac Shakur's father, Billy Garland, lost contact with the family when Shakur was five years old. Shakur thought Garland was dead until he met him again at age 23.

this group came to be known, faced a total of 156 criminal charges, including plans to blow up subways and police stations, five department stores, and the New York Botanical Garden. The group was held in jail on $100,000 bond each, reaching a total of $2.1 million. Afeni Shakur posted bail in January 1970, releasing her from jail until her trial began.

At her trial, Shakur defended herself because she didn't have the money to hire a lawyer. Public defenders are government-paid lawyers who defend people who cannot afford a lawyer, but Shakur refused this service. If the public defender failed, she would be the one to go to jail. She felt she would be more motivated than a public defender to successfully defend her case. Shakur had to conduct her own legal research and interviews, and she had to cross-examine witnesses in the courtroom, including people who worked undercover for the FBI and had infiltrated the Panthers. Under oath in court, these people described illegal FBI wiretaps and admitted to initiating illegal activities. They weren't just observers undercover; they had facilitated crimes for which people like Shakur were arrested. In May 1971, the jury came back with a verdict of not guilty. Shakur was released from jail. One month later, on June 16, 1971, she gave birth to Tupac Shakur in Harlem, New York City.

Tupac's Early Life

When Shakur was 13, his mother moved him and his younger sister, Sekyiwa, from New York City to Baltimore, Maryland. As a student at Roland Park Middle School in Baltimore, Shakur was already into hip-hop. He spent time with a classmate, Dana Smith, listening to all types of music. As they listened, they learned the skills they would need to create their own music. While their classmates played sports, Shakur and Smith wrote rhymes.

After going to Paul Laurence Dunbar High School for his freshman year of high school, Shakur wanted to attend the Baltimore School for the Arts, a free magnet school. But that

NAMES

Before she changed her own name, Afeni Shakur was called Alice Faye Williams. Tupac Shakur's name was initially Lesane Parish Crooks, but his mother wanted him to have the name of a strong leader, so she later changed his name to Tupac Shakur. When European colonists enslaved people from Africa, the Africans lost their names and much of their cultures, being forced to use the names given to them by white slaveholders. Members of the Black Panthers chose their own names as a symbolic way to reclaim the power that was taken from their enslaved ancestors. Tupac Shakur's mother named him after Tupac Amaru II, a Peruvian revolutionary who fought against the Spanish in the 1700s. In his rap career, Shakur sometimes stylized his name as 2Pac.

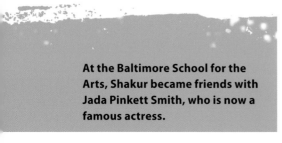
At the Baltimore School for the Arts, Shakur became friends with Jada Pinkett Smith, who is now a famous actress.

meant having to audition. When he lived in New York, Shakur had been in a community theater production of *A Raisin in the Sun* by Lorraine Hansberry, so he chose this play for his audition. Smith ran through lines of dialogue with him. Shakur's audition was a success, and he was accepted into the school as a theater major starting his sophomore year.

As a theater student, Shakur studied the plays of William Shakespeare and Henrik Ibsen. He learned ballet, and he was a skilled actor. But he was never tempted to focus on anything but rap. He wrote poetry, honing his rhyming skills.

While friends like Smith had money from their families, Shakur's family was always poor. After a neighborhood boy was killed in a gang shooting, Afeni Shakur grew worried for her children's safety, so she sent them to live with a friend in California. She joined them shortly after. It was around this time that Afeni Shakur started using crack cocaine. Young Tupac Shakur sold the drug to help support his family.

Breaking into the Music Industry

In early 1989 in California, when Shakur was 17 years old, he met Leila Steinberg, an activist and teacher. They started talking about Winnie Mandela, a South African activist, and Shakur's poetry. The two became friends. At that time, Steinberg had no experience in the music industry, but Shakur eventually convinced her to become his manager.

Steinberg wasn't able to get Shakur a recording contract, but she did get him a meeting with music manager Atron Gregory. She called Gregory and told him that Shakur would one day sell more albums than any other rapper, something that Shakur himself had originally told Steinberg. Gregory was intrigued by Shakur's confidence. In 1990, Gregory gave Shakur a job as a dancer and a roadie, hauling and setting up equipment with the hip-hop group Digital Underground, a group Gregory managed. The group gave Shakur an opportunity to record his own song, and he made his debut in

Early in his career, Shakur, *right*, met several famous rappers including Flavor Flav, *left*.

Shakur became known for rapping about racial injustice and other social issues.

1991 with "Same Song," which became part of the soundtrack of the comedy movie *Nothing but Trouble*. That same year, Shakur was featured on Digital Underground's album *Sons of the P.* Soon, Gregory took over managing the young rapper. In November 1991, Shakur released his own album, *2Pacalypse Now.*

The album was a dream come true for Shakur. The rapper was generous with the money he earned and gave back to his community throughout his career. He hired his friend Molly Monjauze to handle his donations to community projects. Shakur financed sports teams in South Central Los Angeles and a center for at-risk youth, and he also paid for a toll-free phone number that kids could call to discuss their problems with him.

Shakur and the Law

But Shakur's early success in rap came with a price. In August 1992, while Shakur was posing for photos and signing autographs at a festival in his Marin City, California, neighborhood, he was assaulted by a group of young men. Shakur carried a pistol for self-defense, and the gun fell to the ground in the struggle. When someone else grabbed it, the gun went off. Qa'id Walker-Teal, a six-year-old who just happened to be nearby, was shot and killed. Shakur didn't face criminal charges, but he was distraught. In 1995, Walker-Teal's family sued Shakur, but they settled out of court, with the boy's family reportedly receiving between $300,000 and $500,000.[1]

The shooting was not the last of Shakur's problems with violence or the law. In 1993, while driving in Atlanta, Georgia, where he was scheduled to perform, Shakur saw two white men arguing with an African American driver. Shakur stopped,

CIVIL LAWSUIT

While no criminal charges were filed against Shakur in Walker-Teal's death, the boy's family filed a civil lawsuit against Shakur. In a criminal case, someone has broken a law and can go to prison if found guilty. In a civil case, a person who is found guilty has to pay a fine to the people who filed the suit. A criminal case is usually settled by a jury. Not all civil cases go before a jury, and there generally does not have to be as much evidence to win this kind of case, compared with a criminal case.

23

and the argument escalated. Shakur and one of the white men fired gunshots. Both of the white men got shot, and Shakur was arrested for aggravated assault. But police investigating the case discovered that the men, brothers Mark and Scott Whitwell, were off-duty police officers who had been drinking, and the gun one of them carried had been stolen from a police evidence locker. The charges against Shakur were dropped.

In November 1993, Shakur was arrested on suspicion of sexual abuse. A group of men had raped a 19-year-old fan in Shakur's hotel suite in New York. Shakur had been in the hotel room. He denied committing a crime, but the woman said Shakur contributed to the sexual assault. "[Shakur] took

Shakur was arrested in Manhattan, New York, for sexual abuse in November 1993.

advantage of his stardom to abuse me and betray my trust," the young woman said during the rapper's trial in 1994.[2] She testified that after being forced to have sex with the group of men, she frequently had nightmares. She also received a number of anonymous threatening phone calls.

Shakur later admitted to *Vibe* journalist Kevin Powell that he could have prevented the rape but didn't. "I had a job," Shakur said, "and I never showed up."[3] The only two people charged in the case were Shakur and his road manager, Charles Fuller, who reportedly did not touch the victim but also allowed the rape to happen. Both Shakur and Fuller were convicted of first-degree sexual abuse. Shakur was sentenced to up to four and a half years in prison, having to serve at least eighteen months before being eligible for parole. Shakur was eventually released from prison with the help of Interscope Records, which paid a $1.4 million bond for him.

FULLER'S PENALTY

For his part in the sexual assault case, Charles Fuller received a lighter prison sentence than Shakur. Judge Daniel P. Fitzgerald said Fuller was guilty because he had set up the meeting that led to the rape, and he had stood by while the assault occurred. But the judge gave Fuller a lighter sentence than Shakur because Fuller had no criminal record. Shakur had been arrested six times preceding the trial for various reasons, including weapons charges and assault. Fuller received four months in jail and five years' probation.

CHAPTER THREE

BIGGIE SMALLS

Twenty-one years before Shakur and Smalls would meet, Biggie Smalls was born Christopher George Latore Wallace on May 21, 1972, in Brooklyn, New York, to parents who were both Jamaican immigrants. His mother, Voletta Wallace, was a preschool teacher who moved to the United States as a teenager. She gave birth to Smalls when she was 24. His father, Selwyn Wallace, was a welder and a politician in the local Jamaican community. Selwyn Wallace left the family when Smalls was two years old.

Because of this, Voletta Wallace worked two jobs to support the family. She told a reporter from the *Guardian* newspaper in 1999 that she and Smalls had everything they needed. They lived in a seven-room apartment in Brooklyn's Bedford-Stuyvesant neighborhood. "We were never hungry or in need of clothing. I'm sure he was in need of the Versaces, the Chanels and the Guccis, but I wouldn't buy them for him.

Biggie Smalls, who professionally rapped as The Notorious B.I.G., performs in 1994.

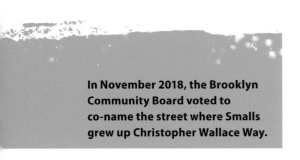

In November 2018, the Brooklyn Community Board voted to co-name the street where Smalls grew up Christopher Wallace Way.

I believe if you want it, you work for it and buy it yourself," she told the *Guardian*.[1] Speaking to the reporter, Wallace portrayed herself as a strict parent with basic house rules pasted to the apartment door. She didn't allow smoking or hats to be worn indoors. If someone broke something, it was their job to fix it. Even grammar was included in the rules—Wallace wanted to hear "May I?" instead of "Can I?"[2]

School Days

A big part of why Wallace worked two jobs was so she could send Smalls to private Catholic schools. In middle school, he went to Queen of All Saints Academy. He achieved good grades, but he was also selling drugs, using the income to purchase the designer gear his mother wouldn't buy for him. Wallace knew other kids made fun of her son's school uniforms, but she didn't know that he was selling drugs to pay for new clothes.

Smalls started high school at Bishop Loughlin Memorial High School, where he excelled in English classes. He had already started rapping to entertain his neighbors, and he realized that if he wanted to focus on rap, attending the Catholic college-prep school wouldn't be the best path.

Because of this, he transferred to George Westinghouse Career and Technical Education High School in Brooklyn.

Westinghouse proved to be a good choice. Smalls went to school with other future famous rappers DMX, Jay-Z, and Busta Rhymes. Busta Rhymes and Jay-Z even had a rap battle at school. Years later, Rhymes had no problem admitting that Jay-Z won. "I got to give it up. . . . That was probably the first time that I lost a battle that mattered. [Jay-Z] always exemplified greatness as an MC," Rhymes said in 2010.[3] The rappers' competition was friendly, not fierce. The four influenced each other musically, and after high school, once they were successful rappers, they featured each other on various songs. Despite having these musically collaborative

DMX, JAY-Z, AND BUSTA RHYMES

DMX, Busta Rhymes, and Jay-Z, who all went to school with Smalls, also went on to have successful rap careers. Jay-Z, born Shawn Corey Carter in 1969, has recorded numerous popular singles, including collaborations with his wife, pop superstar Beyoncé. As president of Def Jam records, Jay-Z has also signed high-impact acts like Rihanna. In June 2019, *Forbes* magazine reported Jay-Z had become a billionaire.

DMX was born Earl Simmons in 1970. His first album, *It's Dark and Hell Is Hot*, debuted at Number 1 on the hip-hop charts in 1998. It sold more than five million copies. His second album, *Flesh of My Flesh, Blood of My Blood*, also debuted at Number 1. DMX is also known for having fun with music, such as rapping "Rudolph the Red-Nosed Reindeer."

Busta Rhymes, born Trevor Smith Jr. in 1972, was in a group called Leaders of the New School before releasing his solo album, *The Coming*, in 1996. He also acts, appearing in a remake of the Hollywood movie *Shaft*, and writes for television.

REALITY OR JUST A STORY?

Rap lyrics are known for telling the stories of impoverished African American people living in inner cities. Voletta Wallace told the *Guardian* that many of Smalls's lyrics may be someone's life story, but they were not her son's reality. "Like he rapped that he was poor and Christmas missed him? Christmas never missed my son," she told the reporter. "As far as the line about the landlord insulting us, I never owed [rent]. Up to this day, my credit is the best in the world. He's telling a story." Wallace still doesn't like the profane language used in her son's raps, but she says that when she looks beyond it, she can see the beautiful stories he told. Still, she has firm opinions about why he told profanity-laced stories of violence. She believes he told the stories that the people who still buy his albums want to hear. "The main buyers of hip-hop: white, middle-class boys excited by the images of a violent African American culture," *Guardian* reporter Raekha Prasad wrote after interviewing Wallace.[4]

friends at school, Smalls dropped out of high school in 1989, when he was 17 years old.

Smalls was also arrested for the first time that same year. After he dropped out of high school, Smalls became more seriously involved in dealing drugs. His first arrest was for carrying a loaded, unregistered gun, and he was sentenced to five years of probation. A year later, he was caught violating this probation. A year after that, he was arrested for dealing crack cocaine in North Carolina. After that arrest, he remained in jail for nine months before making bail.

Making Music

After he got out of jail, Smalls borrowed a friend's recording equipment and cut a demo tape. At this point, he was still going by his birth name, Christopher Wallace. He decided to choose a stage name, calling himself Biggie Smalls, in part because his childhood nickname was "Big." Smalls hadn't previously considered a full-time career in music, but he wanted to do something that would let him showcase his abilities as a writer. People had responded well when they heard him rap for fun, so he decided to try it as a career.

"It was fun just hearing myself on tape over beats," he said in an Arista Records biography.[5] His demo tape found its way to *Source* magazine. The magazine's staff members were so impressed that they profiled him in their March 1992 "Unsigned Hype" column. Because of this profile, he was asked to record with other unsigned rappers. Producer Sean "Puffy" Combs, who today goes by the name "Diddy," heard this recording and decided to pursue Smalls. He signed Smalls for a record deal with Uptown Records. Just a short time later,

BIGGIE SMALLS SUED BIGGIE SMALLS

Although many people still call him Biggie Smalls, Smalls was forced to change his stage name to The Notorious B.I.G. because of a lawsuit. Biggie Smalls was the name of a gang leader in the 1975 movie *Let's Do It Again*. Calvin Lockhart, a Bahamian American actor, played the character but didn't see it as a compliment that the character's name had been used again. Lockhart sued, forcing Smalls to become, at least on stage, The Notorious B.I.G.

Combs left Uptown Records and started his own company, Bad Boy Records. Smalls signed with him there by mid-1992.

Before any of his work with Bad Boy was released, Uptown put out a remix of "Real Love" by Mary J. Blige with a verse by The Notorious B.I.G., Smalls's new stage name. Uptown followed

Smalls, left, with Sean "Puffy" Combs in 1997

T'YANNA WALLACE

Born in 1993, T'yanna Wallace is the daughter of Biggie Smalls and his teen girlfriend Jan Jackson. Jackson and Smalls grew up in the same neighborhood but didn't meet until they were 18 years old. When T'yanna was about eight months old, Jackson and Smalls broke up. T'yanna was three years old when her father was killed. She is now a graduate of Penn State and owns her own streetwear company with a storefront in Brooklyn. "The Wallace name is big, I'm not gonna lie. . . . I try to just continue the legacy. That's why I started my clothing line dedicated to him," T'yanna said in an interview with MusicXclusives TV in June 2016. "I'm not into music, I don't rap or anything, so I was like, let me do something that I love dedicated to him."[7] She named her clothing line Notoriouss in honor of her father, but she doubled the "s," to add her own sense of style.

this with a release of Smalls's solo single, "Party and Bulls***."
These works were released even as he was working on his first full album with Bad Boy. Smalls's daughter was born around this time too.

Smalls's debut album with Bad Boy, *Ready to Die*, marked a resurgence in East Coast hip-hop with multisyllabic rhymes, intricate wordplay, and a fast delivery. Smalls's lyrics were noted for showing emotion and for revealing the stressful side of the drug-dealing lifestyle, which was often portrayed by rappers as glamorous. "In street life you're not allowed to show if you care about something," Combs said to the *New York Times*. "You've got to keep that straight face. The flip side of that is [Smalls's] album. He's giving up all his vulnerability."[6]

CHAPTER FOUR

FRIENDS AND ENEMIES

Smalls visited Los Angeles in 1993 as an unknown rapper. He put the word out that he wanted to meet Shakur. When Shakur heard this, he invited Smalls and his group over to his home. An Uptown Records intern told the *Fader* magazine that the group smoked and drank, and Shakur cooked for everyone. "Pac was like, 'Yo, come get it,' and we go into the kitchen, and he had steaks, and French fries, and bread, and Kool-Aid, and we just sittin' there eating and drinking and laughing. And you know, that's truly where Big and Pac's friendship's started," said intern Dan Smalls, who was not related to the rapper.[1]

When Biggie Smalls returned to the East Coast, he stayed in touch with Shakur, and whenever Smalls was in California, he slept on Shakur's sofa. When Shakur was in New York, he would visit Smalls and throw dice with the guys in the neighborhood.

Shakur, *left*, and Smalls perform together in 1993.

Shakur gave Smalls advice when asked, and the two performed together on one of Shakur's trips to the East Coast, freestyling at a concert in Madison Square Garden in 1993.

Despite his friendship with Shakur, Smalls wasn't well known outside of Brooklyn. Shakur, on the other hand, was a movie star with platinum albums. Shakur was generous with his rap experience, and whenever Smalls and other up-and-coming rappers gathered at recording studios, Shakur gave them advice on how to make a name for themselves. Before Smalls's first album, *Ready to Die*, was released in 1994, he was concerned with how well it would do. Combs's new record label hadn't proven itself yet, so Smalls asked Shakur to replace Combs as his manager. Shakur convinced Smalls that Combs knew what he was doing. "He will make you a star," Shakur said.[2]

Smalls, *left*, and Shakur started out as friends, with Shakur often giving advice to the younger Smalls.

Shakur said he advised Smalls to change his style somewhat to appeal more to female fans. If Smalls did that, Shakur said, young women would buy his albums and their boyfriends would too. As proof that he not only gave this advice but that Smalls listened to it, Shakur would point to the differences between the hard, aggressive "Party and Bulls***" single and the less forceful "Big Poppa" on *Ready to Die.*

Blaming Biggie

This friendship that started because of a love of rap was short-lived. On November 30, 1994, Shakur was in New York, entering Quad Recording Studios on Seventh Avenue. As he, his manager Freddie Moore, and his friend Randy "Stretch" Walker neared the elevators, they were confronted by gunmen. Some sources say there were two gunmen, and some say there were three. The gunmen demanded that Shakur and his companions hand over their money and jewelry. Moore and Walker immediately complied, but Shakur refused and swore at the men. They shot him five times and then stole $40,000 in jewelry from him before Walker could drag Shakur to safety in the elevator.

No one was ever charged in this crime, but Shakur believed he knew who was responsible. In an interview with *Vibe* magazine, he blamed Smalls and Combs. When the magazine article came out in April 1995, *Vibe* had changed the names of

QUAD CONFESSION

Although no one was ever arrested for shooting Shakur at Quad Recording Studios, in 2011, Dexter Isaac, who was jailed in New York for an unrelated crime, confessed to being one of the two gunmen. He claimed that James "Jimmy Henchman" Rosemond paid him to stage the robbery. "He gave me $2,500, plus all the jewelry I took, except for one ring, which he wanted for himself. It was the biggest of the two diamond rings that we took. He said he wanted to put the stone in a new setting for his girlfriend," Isaac said.[3] Despite this confession, no one will be charged with the crime. In New York State, the statute of limitations on a robbery runs out in seven years. That means that after 2001, no one could be charged for this particular crime.

the two people Shakur accused, giving them fake names to protect their identities. But readers quickly figured out that Shakur was talking about Smalls and Combs. Smalls denied this allegation and said that he knew nothing about the shooting.

Shakur's speculations about who was behind the Quad building mugging didn't stop with Smalls and Combs. From an eighth-floor window, rapper Lil' Cease had called out to Shakur as he entered the building. At one point, Shakur claimed Lil' Cease was to blame, but he also accused James "Jimmy Henchman" Rosemond, a well-known drug dealer.

Shakur wasn't alone in speculating about the crime. Other people believed music promoter Jacques "Haitian Jack" Agnant and Walter "King Tut" Johnson, organizer of the Black Mafia robbery ring, had organized the robbery and shooting. It seemed like everyone in the rap community had a theory, but no one was ever arrested in the case. No matter who was behind the robbery and shooting, after this, the rivalry between East Coast and West Coast rappers heated up.

The rivalry wasn't new. Hip-hop started on the East Coast, with artists rhyming about poverty and police brutality. MCs and DJs popularized this new music. On the West Coast, rappers wore plaid shirts and gang colors. Their raps about gang life had a driving funk beat. Early on, West Coast rappers felt their music didn't get the radio time or media attention it deserved on the East Coast. With Shakur and Smalls, this competition grew.

East Coast vs. West Coast

Two months after the shooting at Quad, Biggie released the single "Big Poppa." The B-side to this piece was "Who Shot Ya?" which described Smalls as taking down an opponent. "Who shot ya? Separate the weak from the obsolete," the lyrics say.[4]

VIBE TO BLAME?

Vibe editors would later admit that their April 1995 issue was the first inkling Smalls had that Shakur blamed him and Combs for the Quad shooting. Shakur accused Smalls in the magazine, and reporters did not ask for a comment from Smalls to allow him to defend himself in the same issue. Some journalism experts blame *Vibe* for the split between the rappers. Although the two rappers carry much of the blame by escalating the feud in diss tracks and interviews, uneven reporting likely helped spark the feud when Shakur's one-sided, unsubstantiated allegations went to print without a response from Smalls.

Shakur and his fans perceived this song as a diss track taunting Shakur after the shooting. Smalls denied this, saying the song's release was just poorly timed.

The situation escalated when Shakur released his scathing diss track "Hit 'Em Up." In this rap, Shakur claimed he'd had sex with Faith Evans, Biggie's estranged wife. Like "Who Shot Ya?," "Hit 'Em Up" was a B-side release. It accompanied Shakur's single "How Do You Want It?" However, "Hit 'Em Up" was so popular that it was later rereleased as a single on its own. There was no doubt about what Shakur was claiming in the song, because he called Smalls by name in the lyrics, referred to when Smalls slept on his sofa, and more.

DISS TRACKS

A diss track is a song written to disparage another musical artist or group. Shakur and Smalls are not the only artists known for having a diss track battle. Perhaps one of the first artists to release a diss track was soul singer Joe Tex in the early 1960s. His song "You Keep Her" was aimed at singer James Brown, who was spending time with Tex's ex-wife. In 1971, Beatles bandmates Paul McCartney and John Lennon engaged in a similar battle. In "Too Many People," released in 1971, McCartney criticized Lennon's public preaching. Lennon returned fire in 1971 with "How Do You Sleep?" in which he said McCartney's musical career was over. Diss tracks still come out on a regular basis. Rappers Eminem and Machine Gun Kelly released songs dissing each other in 2018. Eminem's song "Killshot," a response to Kelly's "RAP DEVIL," mocked Kelly's beard and his music. Only fans can say whether these tracks build a career or simply show the artist's petty side.

A 1994 issue of *Vibe* magazine features Shakur. Some people blame *Vibe* and other media for fueling the East Coast vs. West Coast rap rivalry.

The song fueled a public rivalry between Shakur and Smalls that reverberated throughout the rap community. When asked in 2018 about "Hit 'Em Up," rapper Eminem said, "Most of it . . . was personal, below-the-belt jabs . . . but it was done so well and the record was just so crazy. The 2Pac-Biggie thing was tough because you liked them both. You were stuck in this weird thing where you were bumpin' a 2Pac diss record, then you were bumpin' something from Biggie that might be dissing [2Pac] in it."[5]

In addition to dissing Smalls, Shakur also dissed East Coast artists Jay-Z, the Fugees, Nas, Junior M.A.F.I.A., Mobb Deep, and Chino XL.

Hip-hop journals wrote about this rivalry, framing it as East Coast vs. West Coast. In doing so, they ignored collaborations between artists from opposite coasts, including Tha Alkaholiks working with New York producer Diamond D on their album

FAITH EVANS

Faith Evans gave her account of what happened between her and Shakur in her memoir, *Keep the Faith*. Evans had gone to Death Row Records to record vocals for Shakur's song "Wonda Why They Call U B****." After the recording had been made, as Evans went to collect her $25,000 check, Shakur asked her to have sex with him. "He asked in a very surprising and offensive way for sure," Evans said. "That is totally not how I operate, that ain't how I do business and that was never up for discussion."[6] Nothing ever happened between the two, according to Evans, regardless of what Shakur later claimed in his rap.

Shakur and Smalls made music about many issues—but a theme that began to emerge was diss tracks, particularly against each other.

Coast to Coast. Instead, the media focused on anything that illustrated and stoked the tension. For example, in August 1996, *Vibe* ran the sensational cover headline "East vs. West: Biggie & Puffy Break Their Silence."[7] Meanwhile, Shakur and Biggie continued to criticize each other on recordings and in interviews. A month later, Shakur was shot to death.

CHAPTER FIVE

FROM SHAKUR'S DEATH TO SMALLS'S DEATH

When Shakur was killed and no one was arrested, the media ran with the story, casting blame on several different people. One of these people was Biggie Smalls, Shakur's former friend turned fierce rival. But Smalls said from the start that he'd had nothing to do with the shooting.

Smalls wasn't the only one who insisted he was innocent of any wrongdoing in Shakur's death. Friends and family backed up his claims of innocence. Talent manager Wayne Barrow told MTV, "I was actually with Big." He said that on September 7, 1996, Smalls was in Combs's recording studio in New York. "'Nasty Girls' is the record we was recording. Him being able to be in two places at one time, he must be a genie," Barrow said.[1]

Smalls always maintained that he was not involved in the shooting of Shakur.

Evans also spoke to MTV, talking about when Smalls had called her with the news. "I was living in Manhattan. I was about eight months pregnant with our son C. J. . . . . I know for a fact he was in Jersey. He called me crying because he was in shock. I think it's fair to say he was probably afraid," Evans said.[2] She explained that Smalls had feared for his own life because his name had been linked to Shakur in negative ways, and Shakur had been murdered.

But Smalls also worried about the impact that he and Shakur had on the rap community as a whole. They had helped create a fierce feud, and after Shakur's death, Smalls felt that something needed to change. Even without Shakur to help, Smalls felt he would have to make that change happen.

Biggie in L.A.

On February 12, 1997, Smalls and California rapper Snoop Dogg declared a truce in the East Coast vs. West Coast rivalry.

"This is strictly for the kids that support our music and support us in general and look up to us and say, 'Well, hey, they not tripping, so we stop tripping,'" Snoop Dogg said.[5] Some people thought the truce might just be a publicity stunt because Smalls and Snoop Dogg declared it at a press conference in Los Angeles before a taping of *The Steve Harvey Show*, which featured the two rappers as guest stars. In the sitcom, actor and TV personality Steve Harvey played a vice principal who, because of budget cuts, also had to teach class. Smalls and Snoop Dogg appeared in the episode taped the same day as their press conference to deliver a message about peace to the class taught by Harvey's character.

The appearance with Snoop Dogg wasn't Smalls's only step toward peace. Almost two weeks later, on February 24, 1997, Smalls appeared on the TV show *Rap City*, interviewed by host

SNOOP DOGG

In 1996, Snoop Dogg was a father with another child on the way. Some journalists, including Cherise Johnson, think that this helped shift his focus to end the rivalry between East and West. "I'm trying to live, y'all n***** trying to die," he said about Knight and others at Death Row Records, although at that time, Snoop was still a Death Row artist.[6] Snoop Dogg contacted Knight, who was in jail, and asked, "Cuz, why don't you let me shake Biggie and Puffy's hand on TV and end this so we can figure out a way to move forward?"[7] Not only did Knight and others at Death Row disagree, but they took personal offense at Snoop Dogg's desire to make peace with Smalls and Combs. After this, Snoop said, their attitude toward him changed. But despite this, Snoop Dogg still appeared in public with Combs and Smalls.

Joe Clair. In the interview, which aired on BET on March 12, 1997, Smalls discussed why he had quit recording diss tracks about West Coast rappers. Smalls said that he had seen how the disagreement and hard feelings between himself and Shakur had escalated and pulled everyone into a vast rap feud. Smalls felt the need to step back and de-escalate things. He had decided to film a music video on the West Coast, which was why he was in Los Angeles for the interview.

Visiting the West Coast may have been a bad decision. James Prince, the CEO of Rap-A-Lot Records, had contacted Smalls and Combs to say that he had heard a lot of talk around L.A. about a possible revenge hit on the two of them. Prince

In 2015, Snoop Dogg wore a T-shirt that depicted Shakur and Smalls with the words *Legends Never Die* to honor the deceased rappers.

hadn't heard specific plans, but he urged Smalls and Combs to take the threats seriously because people were still angry about Shakur's death. Smalls and Combs ignored his concerns and went back to work on the video for "Hypnotize."

Prince wasn't the only one who thought they should be worried. "Anybody in their right mind knew they didn't let enough time pass," said promoter Doug Young.[8] He said Smalls and his crew working in L.A. and staying in a top hotel made it look like they were trying to take Shakur's place. Their presence could have easily sent the wrong message.

On March 7, 1997, Smalls was onstage at the Soul Train Music Awards in Los Angeles to present the award for Best R&B Single. When he called out, "What's up, Cali?" rappers in the audience booed their East Coast rival.[9] Regardless of whether Smalls was trying to make peace, the California rappers were not going to be won over easily.

At the Soul Train Music Awards, Smalls presented the award for Best R&B Single to Toni Braxton for the song "You're Makin' Me High."

The Murder of Biggie Smalls

The day after the awards, on March 8, 1997, Smalls attended a Soul Train after-party at the Petersen Automotive Museum in Los Angeles. Smalls almost didn't go because he was leaving the next morning on a trip to London, England, which Combs had arranged to promote Smalls's work. But Smalls decided to go to the party at the museum because, given the number of celebrities that would be there, he knew it would offer networking opportunities that could help his career. The party was more comfortable for Smalls than the awards ceremony, partly because the DJ, from New York, played not only Smalls's "Hypnotize" but also other Bad Boy Records songs.

After the party, Smalls, Combs, and the Bad Boy entourage left in three vehicles. The first was driven by Combs. Smalls rode in the front passenger seat of the second car. Reggie Blaylock, a police officer who had been hired for the night as a security guard, drove the third vehicle. Traffic was heavy that night, and the cars inched down the street. Combs made it through a red light that stopped Smalls's car.

As Smalls's Suburban sat at the red light, a green Chevy Impala pulled up alongside it. A gunman inside the

SOUL TRAIN AWARDS

In 1997, the same year that Smalls was booed at the Soul Train Awards, Shakur was declared a winner, even after his death. *All Eyez on Me*, Shakur's fourth studio album—the last one he had released during his lifetime—won the Soul Train R&B/Soul or Rap Album of the Year award. The win wasn't entirely surprising, as the album had sold 566,000 copies the week it was released, taking it to Number 1 on the *Billboard* 200 and the R&B/Hip-Hop Albums charts.[10]

Impala fired approximately six shots into the passenger side of the Suburban.[11] Combs jumped out of his car and ran back to Smalls, who had been hit four times in his arm, back, thigh, and hip. One of the shots damaged vital internal organs—his liver, one of his lungs, and his heart. Smalls was losing consciousness when Combs reached his side.

Meanwhile, the Impala carrying the shooter had driven away. The third car from the entourage, driven by Officer Blaylock, was in pursuit. But with the heavy traffic, Blaylock was unable to keep up, and the Impala got away.

Smalls was rushed to Cedars-Sinai Medical Center. When he arrived, his heart had already stopped beating. Smalls was pronounced dead shortly after 1:00 a.m. on March 9, 1997.[12]

Many friends and fans lined the streets of Smalls's neighborhood to mourn the slain rapper during his funeral procession on March 18, 1997.

THE MUSIC OF TUPAC AND BIGGIE

2Pacalypse Now. Released 1991. Peaked at #64 on April 18, 1992.

Ready to Die. Released 1994. Peaked at #15 on October 1, 1994.

Strictly 4 My N..*.*.*.Z.* Released 1993. Peaked at #24 on March 6, 1993.

Died March 9, 1997.

Life after Death. Released 1997. Peaked at #1 on April 12, 1997.

Me against the World. Released 1995. Peaked at #1 on April 1, 1995.

Born Again. Released 1999. Peaked at #1 on December 25, 1999.

All Eyez on Me. Released 1996. Peaked at #1 on March 2, 1996.

Duets: The Final Chapter. Released 2005. Peaked at #1 on January 7, 2006.

Died September 13, 1996.

The Don Killuminati: The 7 Day Theory. Released 1996. Peaked at #1 on November 23, 1996.

Tupac Shakur and Biggie Smalls (as The Notorious B.I.G.) recorded these albums, at least in part, before they died. This chart does not include the many remixes and compilations that have been released subsequently. The rankings come from the *Billboard* Top 100, which notes the 100 top-selling albums each week. The peak listed for each album is its highest point on this *Billboard* chart.

As with the death of Shakur, there were many rumors about who had killed Smalls. Although Suge Knight was in prison at the time for his part in the beating of Orlando Anderson, which violated his parole, some people still believed he was behind Smalls's death. Some, including Faith Evans, blamed the East Coast vs. West Coast rap rivalry and the media that supported it. Others blamed gang warfare.

STILL ON THE CHARTS AFTER DEATH

Although Smalls was working on the song "Nasty Girl" when Shakur was killed, the song was not released until after Smalls's death. Jazze Pha produced the track and lifted Smalls's verse from "Nasty Boy," a track that appeared on Smalls's album *Life after Death*. Others who each contributed a verse to "Nasty Girl" included Combs, Jagged Edge, Nelly, and Avery Storm. "Nasty Girl" peaked at Number 44 in the United States but became Smalls's first Number 1 track in the United Kingdom.[13]

Even as police worked to uncover the killer, fans were able to experience Smalls's music through albums produced after the rapper was killed. These posthumous albums include music that was recorded but not released before Smalls's death. His album *Born Again*, released in 1999, included Smalls's recorded verses with new beats and guest singers. Smalls continues to entertain his fans, even after his death.

CHAPTER SIX

THE INVESTIGATIONS

When police investigate a murder, such as that of Smalls or Shakur, they gather two types of evidence. One is forensic evidence, or physical evidence. This is what is left behind when a crime is committed. This type of evidence can include casings ejected from a gun or the bullet that killed someone. Forensic evidence can also include fingerprints or even DNA, a person's unique genetic signature, which can be derived from hair, blood, or another bodily material left at a crime scene.

The second type of evidence is witness statements. Police talk to people who were around when the crime happened, asking what they saw. If a car was involved in the crime, such as during a drive-by shooting, police will ask witnesses if they can identify the type of car or if they got the license plate number. Witnesses are also asked to describe possible suspects. In the murders of Shakur and Smalls, the police recovered bullets from

A forensics officer collects a shell casing from the scene of a shooting.

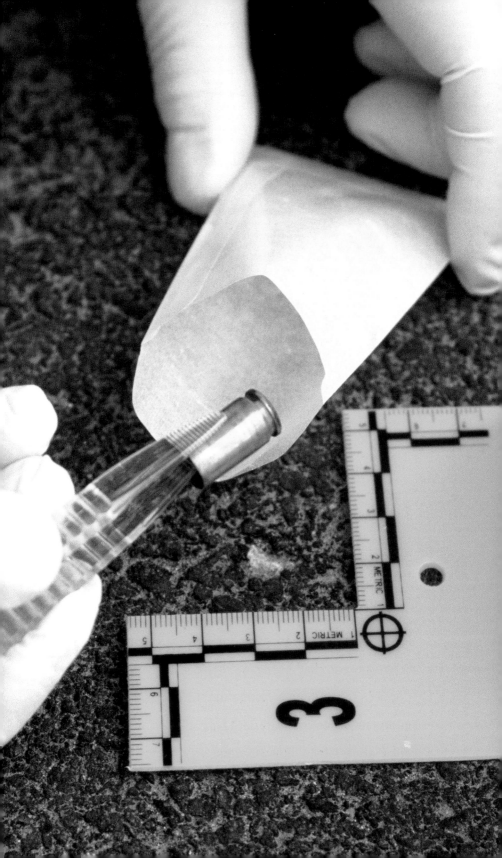

both shootings, but no one the officers talked to would identify either killer.

Many murder cases are never solved. A 2019 study by *BuzzFeed News* found that when a murder victim is Hispanic or African American, police find the killer only 35 percent of the time. The success rate climbs to 54 percent when the victim is white.[1]

Like many murder victims' families, Smalls's family felt that the police were not doing everything they could to solve the case. Voletta Wallace, Faith Evans, and Smalls's children, T'yanna Wallace and C. J. Wallace, filed multiple civil lawsuits against the Los Angeles Police Department. The first lawsuit, filed in 2002, claimed that specific police officers had been involved in the shooting and that the department had failed in its investigation. The judge deciding the civil case declared a mistrial in 2005 when attorneys working for Smalls's family found that the city had withheld documents important to the case. The court ordered the city to pay $1 million in fees.

The family refiled the suit in 2007, but it was again dismissed in 2010. At that time, attorneys for the family and the city agreed that dismissing the lawsuit could make it easier for police to continue investigating the shooting in hopes of finding the killer. The attorneys agreed the lawsuit could be refiled again later. Bradley C. Gage, an attorney representing

Smalls's estate, said the family was not filing these lawsuits for money but for justice. "They want to find the killer or killers and have those people put behind bars. That can help them to put this tragic situation behind them," Gage said.[2]

The police investigating Smalls's death, along with those investigating Shakur's death, insisted they followed every possible lead. But they said many external factors had

Smalls's mother, Voletta Wallace, speaks at a press conference in 2005 after the lawsuit filed by her family was declared a mistrial.

impeded their ability to find answers. Witnesses may refuse to share information with police because they fear gang retaliation, because they do not want to expose their own criminal activity, or because they simply do not trust the police. Also, it can take months or even years for a piece of evidence to surface.

Identifying the Gun

The TV network A&E produced the 2017 documentary *Who Killed Tupac?* The documentary revealed that the gun used in Shakur's death had been found in May 1998 in a backyard in Compton, California. When it was found, Compton police didn't know it was the weapon that had killed Shakur; officers simply catalogued the gun as evidence and stored it. In 2000, the Los Angeles County Sheriff's Department took over policing Compton, and 3,800 firearms catalogued in evidence were transferred to the sheriff's department.[3]

MATCHING THE GUN TO THE BULLET

When technicians have a bullet that is evidence from a crime, they can match it to the gun that fired it. When police find a gun that was possibly used in a crime, such as the gun that may have shot Shakur, the weapon is taken to a forensic laboratory. There, it is fired into a water-recovery tank. The bullet fired from that shot is compared with the bullet recovered from the crime scene. To make this comparison, the technician uses a special microscope that allows both bullets to be viewed at the same time. The technician is looking for telltale marks. As a bullet passes down the barrel of a gun, the grooves in the gun barrel, called rifling, leave distinct marks on the bullet. Using this technique, a technician could tell if a bullet recovered from Shakur or Smalls had been fired by a specific gun.

In 2006, Deputy T. Brennan of the sheriff's department was working on the investigation into Smalls's death. He was reviewing records and realized that he knew the address where this particular gun had been found. It had been the home of a prominent Crips member's girlfriend. Brennan retrieved the gun and ran a ballistics test on it. According to A&E, the test proved it was the gun that had killed Shakur.

The TV network then contacted the Las Vegas Police Department, which had investigated Shakur's murder. According to the documentary, a representative of this department said they had never received the gun from the sheriff's department. The weapon seemed to have gone missing. When evidence goes missing, people grow suspicious that authorities are hiding something.

TROUBLED 1990s

While many African Americans had distrusted the Los Angeles police for decades, events in the 1990s brought a national spotlight on corruption within the LAPD. In 1991, a group of officers were caught on tape beating Rodney King, a man they'd pulled over for speeding. Although the beating led to some departmental reforms, the officers involved were not convicted. This angered many in the African American community, who saw King's beating as a deep injustice, and led to the 1992 Los Angeles riots, during which 63 people died. LAPD Chief Daryl Gates was forced to retire, and Willie Williams became the department's first African American police chief.

Another sign of LAPD corruption came in 1997, when off-duty officer David Mack robbed a bank in South Central Los Angeles, taking $722,000.[4] He had inside help from his girlfriend, the bank's assistant manager Errolyn Romero. In 1998, another incident occurred when Officer Rafael Perez signed six pounds of cocaine out of evidence using another officer's name. His girlfriend then sold the cocaine. When Perez was caught, he cut a deal with police investigators by telling them everything he knew about corruption within the police department, including the shooting of unarmed people, planted guns, and planted drugs. This brought the FBI in to investigate the department.

Crooked Cops?

Media reports of the missing gun weren't the only cause for concern. Los Angeles Police Department officer Russell Poole was a lead investigator on the case of Smalls's murder. He said he found evidence connecting the police department to Death Row Records and Knight. Poole believed Knight had planned Smalls's murder in retaliation for Shakur's murder. Poole was pulled off the case, and he later retired in 1999. Poole had been in contact with the Los Angeles County Sheriff's Department to discuss suspicions that the Los Angeles Police Department had not seriously investigated Smalls's murder because of its ties to Death Row and Knight. He died of a heart attack in 2015 before he could finish writing a book about Smalls's murder.

Poole may have been right to be suspicious. The Los Angeles Police Department was also investigated by the FBI. Phil Carson was an FBI agent assigned to investigate corruption within the police department. At home one evening, he saw a documentary, VH1's *Behind the Music: Notorious B.I.G.*, which included information about Smalls's murder. Carson realized the methods used to kill Smalls would be used by someone familiar with law enforcement procedures. In addition, the murder looked very similar to crimes committed by several officers he had investigated. Carson knew that two of these officers, David Mack and Rafael Perez, had connections to Knight and Death Row Records. Eventually, the FBI closed this investigation because agents felt there wasn't sufficient evidence to charge the officers with Smalls's killing.

Despite years of investigation, the cases of Smalls's and Shakur's murders both remain open. A murder case is usually only closed when a suspect is identified and, if possible, arrested. An example of a case in which a suspect cannot be arrested would be when the suspect has died. With no one arrested, fans and other interested people have developed many theories about who killed the two rappers.

CHAPTER SEVEN

GANG VIOLENCE

There are numerous theories surrounding the deaths of Shakur and Smalls, including many that involve gang violence. In 2017, an anonymous person who worked for the police department told *People* magazine that Shakur's murder happened because of gangs. "It was a gang retaliation murder," he said.[1] He then went on to explain that because Shakur worked with Knight, he was affiliated with Mob Piru. This meant that he was automatically an enemy of the Crips.

In some of his raps, Shakur glamorized the life of a "player," a tough gangster showing off his money. But in other songs, often pieces on the same album, he sang about street life as being desperate, self-destructive, full of fear, and often cut short.

Perhaps it was because Shakur saw this desperation that he was willing to help arrange the Watts gang truce in 1992. In the early 1990s, various gangs controlled territory throughout

Although some of Shakur's rap lyrics portrayed gang violence, Shakur also spoke out against that violence.

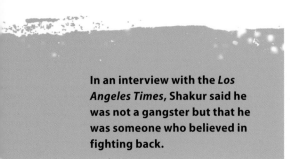
In an interview with the *Los Angeles Times*, Shakur said he was not a gangster but that he was someone who believed in fighting back.

the Watts neighborhood of southern Los Angeles. People, even non-gang members, who wanted to use a gym had to contact the gang who controlled it to get permission. Shakur put those interested in making a truce in touch with Black Panther members, including his stepfather, Mutulu Shakur, who helped write the terms of the truce. Also including rules about not dealing drugs to children or pregnant women, the truce set up a code of conduct for gang members and allowed people to move more safely through Watts.

Despite his work to reduce gang violence, Shakur was pulled into the gang life. Allen and Albert Hughes are film directors who had worked with Shakur and initially found him

THUG LIFE

In 1992, around the same time he was first seen with gang members and wearing gang colors, Shakur started getting tattoos. Tattoos are popular now, but they were less common when Shakur started getting them. One tattoo in particular convinced people that Shakur was in a gang—the words *THUG LIFE* were tattooed on his stomach. But Shakur said *THUG LIFE* actually stood for "The Hate U Give Little Infants F**** Everybody."[2] It was a call to end violence and inequality. "I'm thugging against society. I'm thugging against the system that made me," Shakur said.[3] The Watts truce was also known by some as Thug Life, a call for gang members who lived in the area to quit inflicting violence on each other.

fun and funny. But all of that changed in early 1992, according to Allen Hughes, after Shakur saw a screening of the film *Juice*. Shakur acted in the film, playing the character

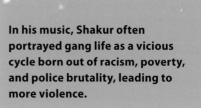

In his music, Shakur often portrayed gang life as a vicious cycle born out of racism, poverty, and police brutality, leading to more violence.

Bishop, a young man from Harlem out to earn respect on the streets. Not long after the screening, according to Allen Hughes, Shakur began hanging out with various gang members. Shakur was photographed in both red and blue bandanas, the gang colors of the Bloods and the Crips respectively, seeming to initially not pick a side.

Mob Piru

Though Shakur was not aligned with one gang or another, that changed when he signed with Knight and Death Row Records. Death Row was connected to Mob Piru, which meant Shakur was also allied with the Mob Piru and affiliated with the Bloods. The Crips had become his enemies.

Early in the day that Shakur was shot, Orlando Anderson, a member of the Crips, saw someone wearing a Death Row Records medallion at a Las Vegas mall. The man wearing the medallion was a Mob Piru member and part of Shakur's entourage. Anderson tried, but failed, to steal the medallion.

BISHOP

Bishop, the character that Shakur played in *Juice*, seemed similar to Shakur in many ways. Journalist Nathan Rabin wrote about this in a 2019 *Vanity Fair* article. In the movie, when Bishop is with his family, he is a good son and grandson. When approached by members of a gang, he morphs into someone who is tough but restrained. A third personality comes out when he sees his friends. "At this point, Bishop morphs instantly into the 2Pac of the popular imagination, a brash, aggressive, irreverent wild card for whom smack-talking came as easily as breathing," Rabin wrote. "Bishop turns tough and defiant because he knows his crew will back him up in a fight but also because he now has an audience to play to."[4] Whether he showed himself as a talented actor and musician or as a tough gang member, Shakur's personality seemed to change with his companions.

Because it involved two gang members, it wasn't just a failed robbery—retaliation was expected.

That evening, Shakur heard that Anderson was at the MGM Grand casino following Tyson's boxing match against Seldon. Shakur rushed over. Soon, a fistfight was underway, with Anderson down on the floor.

A member of the Los Angeles Police Department said a Crips leader had told him that Shakur's death was revenge. According to the officer's story, he was told, "It was simple retaliation: you mess with one of ours, we will mess with one of yours. If Orlando had never been jumped in the hotel, they never would have killed Tupac that night."[5]

Some people believe Shakur, *left*, may have been shot because of his association with Knight, *right*, who was connected to the Mob Piru gang.

Naming Orlando Anderson

Numerous people have publicly claimed that Anderson killed Shakur. In 2018, BET showed an episode of the TV show *Death Row Chronicles* in which Crips member Duane Keith "Keefe D" Davis said he was riding in the car from which the gunshots were fired. In this interview, he refused to say who specifically had fired the shots, only that the shots had come from the vehicle's back seat. But earlier, Davis had told authorities that his nephew, Anderson, had the gun.

Another person who accused Anderson of killing Shakur initially approached the police anonymously, using only the name "Candy." She turned out to be Anderson's aunt. She was willing to help the police because she was not part of a gang,

WHAT SELLS

In many of his songs, Shakur condemned racial injustice and the agonies of urban poverty. One focus was the shooting death of Latasha Harlins, a Los Angeles high school student whose killer was given probation. The fact that the shooter was not sentenced to prison was seen by many as an injustice by the court system. Shakur dedicated "Keep Ya Head Up" to Harlins and mentioned her in "Something to Die 4," "Thugz Mansion," and "I Wonder If Heaven Got a Ghetto." However, some of Shakur's later music focused more heavily on aggressive, gangster-style songs that sold better and were played by mainstream radio stations. These songs included "Ambitionz az a Ridah" and "Hail Mary." They showed the widespread popularity of this type of music even as the violence described in the lyrics was often condemned, even by Shakur himself. In a 1996 interview with *Vibe* magazine, Shakur offered a message to young hip-hop fans: "Because I'm talking about it doesn't mean that it's O.K."[6]

and she believed that Shakur's killing would escalate the already serious gang war in Los Angeles.

Family members were not the only people willing to blame Anderson. Police detective Greg Kading told reporters that a Crips member he called "Brooks" had spoken with police. Brooks said that on the night Shakur had been shot, Anderson was taking credit for the hit.

ANDERSON'S DEATH

Orlando Anderson died on May 29, 1998. His grandmother had died earlier that same day. Anderson told family members that he was going to the store, and then he drove off with friends. Police said that about an hour later, Anderson and a fellow member of the Southside Crips drove to a car wash where members of another gang had gathered. An argument about money broke out, and gunshots were fired. Four men were hit. They were taken to Martin Luther King Jr./Drew Medical Center where Anderson, age 23, and another man were pronounced dead.

People would have had a variety of reasons for turning in Anderson. Some might have truly believed Anderson had committed the shooting and wanted to see justice. Some, like his aunt, wanted to keep a bad situation from getting worse. Still others might have been people arrested for other crimes themselves who offered the police information on Shakur's murder to reduce the charges filed against them. But these weren't the only motives. "Everybody has their own motive, it's not always because you're trying to get yourself out of

Detective Greg Kading, *left*, and Officer Daryn Dupree attended the premiere of *Unsolved*, a TV show about the murders of Shakur and Smalls, in 2018. The show is an example of people's continued interest in the rappers' deaths.

trouble, sometimes it's because you're getting paid. There are informants who do get paid by the police," Kading said.[7] Kading explained that he paid a large number of informants $100 each to find out where drugs were being sold.

Considering that several people approached the police about Anderson, it isn't surprising that people have asked Kading why Anderson was never arrested. "Unfortunately, by the time we had factual proof, Orlando was already dead from an unrelated gang shooting," Kading said.[8] Whatever proof they had must not have been enough to close the case. But Anderson isn't the only possible suspect discussed by conspiracy theorists. Another group of theories revolves around Suge Knight.

CHAPTER EIGHT

SUGE KNIGHT

n 1995, after Shakur was convicted of sexual abuse, he was sent to prison in Dannemora, New York. His mother was about to lose her house because she couldn't make the rent payments. Shakur asked his wife, Keisha Morris, to send a message to Knight saying that he needed help. Although Shakur was not one of Knight's artists, Knight put $15,000 in an account for Shakur to use and started traveling from Los Angeles to Dannemora to see Shakur. Soon, Death Row lawyer David Kenner began working to get Shakur released from prison on an appeal bond, which would allow Shakur to remain out of prison while he waited to see if a court of appeals would overturn the sexual abuse conviction.

On September 16, 1995, Kenner brought a memo to the prison for Shakur to sign. This document both appointed Knight as Shakur's manager and signed Shakur for three albums with Knight's label, Death Row. It should have been considered a

People have several theories about Knight's potential involvement in the murders of both Shakur and Smalls.

conflict of interest that Knight would be Shakur's manager and the owner of the label that produced his records, but Shakur wanted to get out of prison, so he signed the memo. Less than a month later, Interscope Records, which distributed albums for Death Row, posted a $1.4 million bond, and Shakur was released from prison. Shakur always thanked Knight for bailing him out of prison, and Knight took credit for the rapper's release, but the money wasn't his.

Suge Knight, whose legal name is Marion Knight Jr., had a reputation in the music industry. He always looked impressive, often wearing a tailored suit, a square seven-carat diamond earring, and a pinkie ring that spelled out *MOB*. But his reputation was based on much more than his appearance. Knight was also known to be brutal with anyone who opposed or irritated him. This reputation was supported by the legal charges against him. In 1992, he was charged with two counts of assault with a deadly weapon. He had pulled a gun on two rappers, George and Lynwood Stanley, because one of them used a phone at the studio. He hit one of them with the back of the gun, forced them both to their knees, and then made them strip off their pants. He got probation for these charges.

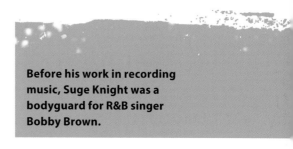

Before his work in recording music, Suge Knight was a bodyguard for R&B singer Bobby Brown.

Considering Knight's reputation, it isn't hard to imagine that someone would want to get revenge on him. One of the theories about Shakur's death is that Shakur wasn't even the intended victim when he was shot. The target may have been Knight.

Knight as the Target

Knight himself is one of the people who believes this theory. He was injured in the shooting, grazed across his forehead by a bullet fragment. Knight has been known to embellish this injury, once insisting that a bullet had embedded itself in his head. In April 2017, Knight had his lawyer draw up a legal document called an affidavit. The document stated that Knight had been the intended victim. It also said the attack was organized by Knight's wife at the time, Sharitha Golden, and the chief of security for Death Row, Reggie Wright Jr.

Golden has given several interviews in which she denies these allegations. "This ridiculous theory that I had to get half of Death Row . . . I already had half of Death Row, America. When Tupac died, what did Death Row become after that? Zero. Nothing. A downfall."[1] As Knight's wife, she already benefitted from Death Row's profits.

Golden also said she is simply not the kind of person who murders other people for financial gain. "I'm such a vicious person, I've adopted a kid, I take care of a disabled person, but I'm a murderer? Come on now," she said sarcastically. "I don't know where America has gone. I don't know why people are so fixated on this murder."[2] Golden asked members of the public to use common sense and think about the people they hurt when they spread rumors and believe every theory they hear.

Did Knight Kill Tupac?

Not every theory that involves Knight casts him in the role of intended

---

SHARITHA GOLDEN

Sharitha Golden worries about the impact that rumors about Shakur's death have had on her children. Golden and Knight have a daughter who cannot post photos of her father on social media without getting comments from her classmates. Golden said, "One minute I've got to deal with my daughter growing up in school and everyone saying her dad killed Tupac, now I've got two other kids in school saying their mom killed Tupac. When does this stop?"[3]

victim. Many people instead believe that Knight ordered someone else to kill Shakur because Shakur wanted to leave Death Row Records. Hopping from one label to another was not unheard of. Still, friends warned Shakur about trying to split from Knight.

Death Row attorney David Kenner represented Shakur in his entertainment contracts and California court cases. But Shakur asked another lawyer, Charles Ogletree Jr., to represent him as well. Ogletree asked to see Shakur's Death Row agreement that he had signed while in prison, but Ogletree was never allowed to see it.

A Death Row Records medallion

WHY KNIGHT WOULDN'T TALK

Some people think Knight's refusal to cooperate with police showed that he was guilty in Shakur's death. A reporter from *Primetime Live*, a news TV show, interviewed Knight in prison and asked him whether he would talk even if he did have information that could lead police to Shakur's killer. "Absolutely not. It's not my job," Knight said. "I don't get paid to solve homicides. I don't get paid to tell on people."[6]

In 1997, Ogletree told the *New Yorker* magazine that Shakur had plans to leave Death Row. Shakur had already formed the production company Euphanasia and had movie deals that were not associated with Death Row. He also had his band, the Outlawz. He had multiple lines of work, which were all part of his supposed plan to leave Death Row. "He had a strategy—the idea was to maintain a friendly relationship with Suge but to separate his business," Ogletree said.[4]

Shakur believed this would be possible because rapper and producer Dr. Dre had already left Death Row, which he had cofounded with Knight and another rapper, The D.O.C. One music business executive told the *New Yorker* that Dre left Death Row because he wasn't comfortable with Knight's "business practices."[5] In order to separate himself from Death Row, Dre agreed to let Knight have the label in return for a small financial settlement. Interscope helped make this deal easier by offering Dre a record deal. "Look at Dre," Ogletree said. "Such a brilliant, creative musician. He started Death Row, and in order to get out he had to give up almost everything. . . . Now, what would it take for Tupac, the hottest star around, whose success was only growing?"[7]

Ogletree knew Shakur could legally leave Death Row. The contract signed in prison would simply have to be renegotiated or challenged in court. But that wasn't the tricky part. "It was a question of how to walk away with your limbs attached and bodily functions operating," Ogletree said.[8] A court could force Knight to separate from Shakur, but even Ogletree expected Knight to retaliate.

Some newspapers called Knight "the most feared man in hip-hop."[9]

In August 1996, Shakur was recording new music and asked Yaasmyn Fula, who ran his company Euphanasia, to pick up the recording tapes so he could listen to them. Death Row staff refused to hand over the tapes, saying that Kenner wouldn't allow it. Although Kenner continued to work for Death Row, Shakur fired Kenner as his own attorney. Ogletree agreed with the firing, but it worried Shakur's more streetwise friends. They believed Kenner's firing would signal to Knight that Shakur was breaking away from Death Row and that Knight would be sure to retaliate. Many people believe Knight responded by having Shakur killed.

Did Knight Kill Biggie?

Other people have theorized that Knight did not kill Shakur but that he killed Smalls in retaliation for the death of Shakur. In some versions of this theory, Knight believed that Smalls had Shakur killed. One person who believes this is Detective Kading. In 2018, Kading did a Reddit AMA (Ask Me Anything), which allowed anyone to send him questions online. Someone wanted to know who killed Smalls. "Suge Knight hired a gang

Knight was arrested in 2015 for hitting two men with his car.

member named Wardell 'Poochie' Fouse," Kading replied, adding that "Biggie was absolutely retaliation for Tupac's murder, so the murders are definitely linked."[10] Kading believes that Smalls had nothing to do with Shakur's death.

Like Anderson, Fouse can no longer be questioned regarding his or Knight's role in the killing of Smalls. On July 24, 2003, Fouse was riding a motorcycle in South Central L.A. when he was shot ten times in his back in what Kading described as infighting between two Blood-related gangs. Fouse died from his injuries.

The conspiracy theories that link Knight to the deaths of Shakur and Smalls may be nothing but wild stories. But either way, Knight is now in prison, serving 28 years for manslaughter in relation to another death. In 2015, Knight was angry about how he had been portrayed in *Straight Outta Compton*, a movie about the late-1980s rap group N.W.A. Knight got into an argument with one of the film's consultants, Cle "Bone" Sloan, at a local restaurant. Knight used his car to hit Sloan and another man, rap music producer Terry Carter, who had worked with Knight. After hitting the men with his car, Knight drove away. Knight later claimed he was in danger and was trying to flee. Sloan was injured, and Carter died. Knight faced charges of murder and attempted murder, but he bargained it down in court to manslaughter, a charge that indicates he did not plan the killing. He began his 28-year prison sentence in 2018.

CHAPTER NINE

SEAN "DIDDY" COMBS

K night is not the only rap icon who is the subject of conspiracy theories surrounding the murders of Shakur and Smalls. Other theories link Sean Combs to the murders. Some blame Combs for Shakur's death. Others say Smalls's killer had actually wanted to shoot Combs, while still others blame Combs for Smalls's death.

In the song "Kill Shot," a September 2018 diss track against fellow rapper Machine Gun Kelly, Eminem mentions Shakur's death and Combs, who now raps under the name Diddy. Eminem rapped, "But, Kells, the day you put out a hit's the day Diddy admits/That he put the hit out that got Pac killed."[1] Eminem said it was a joke. His fans perceived the line this way as well. The meaning of the rap line was obvious to them: Machine Gun Kelly will have a hit song when Combs admits that

Some people believe Sean Combs, Smalls's manager, may have been involved in either Smalls's death or Shakur's.

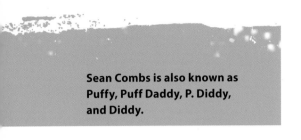

Sean Combs is also known as Puffy, Puff Daddy, P. Diddy, and Diddy.

he killed Shakur, which isn't going to happen because he didn't do it. Just in case all of this wasn't obvious enough, Eminem ended the track with "And I'm just playin', Diddy, you know I love you."[2]

Yet others in the rap community reacted negatively to Eminem's mention of Shakur and Combs. Hip-hop artist Jay Electronica warned Eminem, "You best tread carefully, Son."[3] Former rapper Joe Budden runs *State of the Culture*, a talk show on Revolt TV, Combs's TV network. Budden said that Diddy told him, "Yeah, there's nothing to say about it."[4] Fans also responded on Twitter, with one calling the diss "Baby Lotion Soft."[5]

Stories about this alleged conflict between Eminem and Combs appeared on BET and in magazines. Combs said nothing about the track to mainstream media outlets such as these. Combs's silence made it look like the media was perhaps trying to start a new rap rivalry.

A Contract Hit on Knight and Shakur?

Considering the questions and tensions that still surround the unsolved murders of Shakur and Smalls, it is not surprising that many people protested even a sarcastic mention of the accusation that Combs had killed Shakur. Eminem's diss track was not the first time Combs had been accused of the crime. In 2008, a Los Angeles police task force received a statement from Crips member Duane Keith "Keefe D" Davis. He claimed Combs had offered the Crips a contract for the shooting. Davis is the same person who, in 2018 on an episode of BET's *Death Row Chronicles*, said that he had been riding in the car from which the gunshots were fired at Shakur and implicated his own nephew, Anderson.

In 2008, Davis claimed that Combs had approached him to kill Shakur because the Crips provided security for Combs's Bad Boy label whenever Combs was in Los Angeles. Davis alleged that because of this, Combs had offered the Crips $1 million to have both Knight and Shakur murdered. In his 2011 book

BAD BOY RECORDS

Sean Combs launched Bad Boy Records in 1993. The label has signed musicians from various musical genres, including Biggie Smalls as The Notorious B.I.G., Christian hip-hop artist Mase, gospel singer Mario Winans, rapper Lil Jon, country singer Liz Davis, and pop girl group Danity Kane. It is fitting that this was Smalls's home label, because Combs and Bad Boy have the reputation for "bigger is better."[6] When *National Public Radio* asked Combs why he did things this way, he told them it was to set an example for kids. He said he wanted to show young African Americans, and the world in general, that they should see themselves as having the potential to be successful. "I have to show 'em another image, no matter how it rubs people the wrong way. It's important," Combs said.[7]

Murder Rap, Kading quotes Davis as saying, "[Combs] was like, 'I want to get rid of them dudes.' . . . I was like, 'Man, we'll wipe [them] out, quick . . . it's nothing. Consider that done.'"[8]

There are several reasons to question this story, however. Davis did not approach Kading or anyone else on the task force with this information. Kading, who was investigating Smalls's death, heard that Davis had seen Smalls at the Soul Train after-party shortly before Smalls was killed. Kading wanted to get Davis to talk about who might have killed Smalls. So Kading set up a sting in the form of a drug deal. Once Davis had been arrested and was facing decades in prison, he was more than willing to talk. But he didn't know who had killed Smalls. Instead, Davis told Kading this story about Combs. Davis was facing 25 years in prison if he was convicted on the drug charges, so he may have lied to Kading in an attempt to get leniency.

But that's not the only reason to question Davis's story. As *Forbes* journalist Cathy Scott has pointed out, $1 million is a huge sum of money to pay to have anyone killed. Scott also pointed out that Anderson bragged about shooting Shakur as early as the day after the shooting took place, but he never said a word about the job being a contract killing. Given the unreliable nature of Davis's story, it isn't surprising that Combs denies this allegation.

Combs has had a long, successful career as a rapper, producer, and businessman.

In addition, Combs told *MTV News* that he had never hired the Crips as security:

> But the misconception is that because we're young and we're black, we're not handling business like anybody else. It would be extremely unintelligent to hire gangs to do security. . . . We have never, never hired any gangs for security. As a matter of fact, when we were out there we had off-duty California police officers as security with us that night that [Smalls's murder] happened, also.[9]

Smalls's Death and Combs

Eugene Deal, Smalls's bodyguard the night he was killed, also blames Combs for Smalls's death. But unlike the theory connecting Combs to Shakur's death, Deal does not think Combs had Smalls killed. He thinks that Combs was actually the target.

THE WEIGHT OF GUILT

In 2017, 20 years after Smalls was killed, Combs said, "Time heals all wounds, but this one ain't healed yet."[11] In an interview that was published in *GQ* in 2018, he admitted that he hasn't really dealt with the emotions tied to his friend's death. Smalls had decided to stay in California that night instead of following their original plans, which were for Smalls to fly to London. Combs had tried to persuade Smalls to keep with their plans but eventually backed down. Combs isn't guilty of killing Smalls, but the guilt over this decision is still with him.

Deal, who was the head of security for Bad Boy, told his story in an interview with MReckTV. He said he had heard things that made him think Combs's life was in danger. Deal said that after Smalls's death, he told Combs:

> I told you that these cats were coming to kill us or try to get at us that night. I told you I had intel, but you didn't wanna hear it. Let's reminisce the fact that I told our driver, Kenny, "Run these next three lights. Run the lights, Kenny." Kenny ran the light, Big stopped at the light, Big gets killed. Wasn't meant for him, bruh.[10]

Deal claims that he wanted Combs and Smalls to ride together so that he could more easily watch over the pair, but Combs had insisted on driving separately. Why

Like Shakur, Sean Combs has acted in movies, appearing in *Monster's Ball*, *Get Him to the Greek*, and *Draft Day*.

would Combs not protect Smalls? Some people say Combs wanted Smalls's soon-to-be-released album to sell as well as Shakur's posthumous album. Smalls's forthcoming album was titled, ironically, *Life after Death*. People who blame Combs for supposedly not protecting Smalls say there was more money to be made with Smalls dead, based on the success of Shakur's album after his death. These people also point out that Combs's tribute song to Smalls, "I'll Be Missin' You," hit Number 1.

CHAPTER TEN

MORE CONSPIRACY THEORIES

Christopher French, a professor of psychology at Goldsmiths, University of London, explained to *Scientific American* magazine why people believe conspiracy theories. Humans recognize patterns in the world and then use these patterns to determine cause and effect. The police use patterns in solving crimes, which is how they know what type of tire left a specific track and even that a shattered car window can reveal from which direction a bullet was fired. Sometimes, the desire to find patterns works against people because they discover patterns that aren't actually there. This can happen in several ways.

One of these ways is called confirmation bias. People tend to believe things that confirm how they already see the world.

Fans today still question the murders of Shakur and Smalls, and they honor the rappers in many ways, such as through street art.

Shakur was inducted into the Rock & Roll Hall of Fame in 2017. The music of both Shakur and Smalls has remained influential after their deaths.

People who don't trust the police readily believe that the police or FBI were involved in the deaths of Shakur and Smalls.

Another type of bias is proportionality bias. This is the idea that big events have equally big causes. The loss of two influential musicians has to have a big cause. People who think this way may look for a conspiracy involving a police force or a record label. They may also seek to link the two deaths, making the event even bigger, which would require an even bigger cause. In this way, people developed theories linking the deaths of Shakur and Smalls, although police have never officially found such a link.

People are especially likely to believe in conspiracies when they feel that events are out of their control. Fans of these two musicians often felt a close tie to them and their music. When Shakur and Smalls died and the killers were not found by police, these fans looked for a reason and someone to blame. Some

NONVIOLENT RAP

Rap may have a reputation for being about violence and guns, but not all rappers take that approach. The earliest so-called "clean" rapper may have been Will Smith, who started rapping in the 1980s under the name the Fresh Prince. He has since been joined by Common, who is known for his clean rhymes, and Chamillionaire, who quit using the N-word when he heard white fans repeating it in his song "Ridin." Rapper Lil Mama works to create music that young female fans can relate to. Snoop Dogg has performed gospel under the name Snoop Lion. He made a song with his daughter Cori B called "No Guns Allowed."

people blamed gangs, in part because of rap's violent reputation, and others blamed Knight, Smalls, or Combs. Still others blamed the police or FBI.

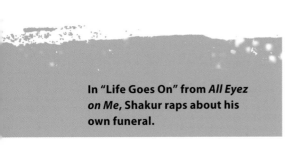

In "Life Goes On" from *All Eyez on Me*, Shakur raps about his own funeral.

FBI to Blame

Several conspiracy theories state that law enforcement is to blame for the murders of Shakur and Smalls. Some of these theories are simple, such as the one that says that the FBI killed both Shakur and Smalls to put an end to violent rap culture. But many of these theories are much more complex.

In 2011, the FBI released a file on Shakur concerning an investigation that had started on September 11, 1996, two days before the rapper died. The file describes a blackmail scheme in which an anonymous person would call Shakur and threaten his life. After this threat was made, members of the Jewish Defense League, which the FBI calls a violent, right-wing domestic terrorist group, would contact him and offer protection for a fee.

Although the FBI investigated this case for three years, the file was closed in 1999. No one was arrested, despite the fact that Shakur had been killed. Failure by the FBI to charge anyone with either threatening, blackmailing, or killing Shakur convinced many people, including fans, that at best, the FBI did not take the threat seriously. At worst, the FBI may have been involved.

Still Alive

Some conspiracy theorists believe Shakur and Smalls are still alive. In part, these theories are based on people's claims that they have seen one of the rappers face-to-face. In 2016, Instagram user Nass Kitojo posted a photo of his bachelor party, complete with a man who looked a lot like Biggie Smalls. In 2012, pop superstar Rihanna posted a photo on Instagram that supposedly showed herself with Shakur. That image can still be found online, but few people do enough research to discover that it is actually a Photoshopped image with Rihanna's face superimposed on Faith Evans's body. In 2016, another photo of Rihanna and Shakur was posted. This, too, was revealed to be

CONSPIRACY THEORY INDUSTRY

The sale of movies, books, and other media about conspiracies has become an industry. People can find books that claim Shakur is still alive. Other books talk about how he was killed by Combs. Still others talk about Shakur predicting his own death. None of the claims can be proven, and very few of the people who write these books make much money, yet conspiracy theories draw a lot of attention.

a Photoshopped image. Still, based on these photos, fans are willing to believe that Shakur is living a secret life in Cuba.

In a September 2017 interview for the documentary *Who Shot Tupac and Biggie?*, Knight revealed that he, too, thinks Shakur might still be alive. "When I left that hospital, me and

While many people have theories about what happened to the rappers, the murders of Shakur and Smalls remain unsolved.

'Pac was laughing and joking. I don't see how someone can go from doing well to doing bad," Knight said.[1] He then added that with Shakur, people never knew what to expect and that he could be somewhere living in secret.

Still Unsolved

Unless new evidence comes to light, the world may never know who really killed Tupac Shakur or Biggie Smalls. As time goes on, solving these crimes seems less and less likely to occur. More people potentially involved in the case die without revealing what they know. Leads grow cold. There are fewer and fewer ways that police can follow up on the information they've already gathered.

Still, the number of people who claim that they know what happened does not seem to be dwindling. In part, this is because people still want to link their names in some way to the names of these influential rappers. Conspiracy theories will survive and continue to thrive as long as these cases remain unsolved.

TIMELINE

1971

- On June 16, Tupac Shakur is born in Harlem, New York.

1972

- On May 21, Christopher George Latore Wallace, later known as Biggie Smalls, is born in Brooklyn, New York.

1991

- Shakur debuts as a rapper with "Same Song." It became part of the soundtrack of *Nothing but Trouble*.

1992

- In August, Shakur is assaulted and drops a gun. When someone grabs for it, the gun goes off, and six-year-old Qa'id Walker-Teal is shot and killed.

- Smalls signs with Sean Combs at Uptown Records.

1993

- Smalls and Shakur meet.

- On August 8, Smalls's first child, daughter T'yanna Wallace, is born.

1994

- Smalls's first album, *Ready to Die*, is released.

- On November 30, Shakur is shot five times at Quad Recording Studios in Brooklyn, New York.

- Shakur is convicted of first-degree sexual abuse.

1995

- In an interview with *Vibe* magazine, Shakur indirectly accuses Combs and Smalls of having something to do with him being shot in November 1994.

1996

- On September 7, Shakur is shot while in Las Vegas, Nevada.

- On September 13, Shakur is taken off life support and dies.

1997

- On February 12, Smalls and Snoop Dogg declare a truce in the East vs. West rap rivalry.

- On March 7, Smalls is booed when presenting at the Soul Train Music Awards in Los Angeles.

- On March 8, Smalls is shot. He dies the next day.

2002

- Smalls's family sues the Los Angeles Police Department over its failure to find out who killed Smalls.

2005

- A judge declares a mistrial in the lawsuit Smalls's family filed against the Los Angeles Police Department.

2007

- Smalls's family refiles the lawsuit.

2010

- The lawsuit is dismissed, lest it interfere in the investigation. The judge says it can be refiled at a later date.

ESSENTIAL FACTS

SIGNIFICANT EVENTS

- On September 7, 1996, Tupac Shakur, Suge Knight, and the Death Row entourage were shot at while driving to a Las Vegas nightclub. Shakur was hit multiple times. He died six days later.

- On March 8, 1997, Biggie Smalls was shot and killed while driving away from a Soul Train Music Awards after party in Los Angeles.

- The murders remain unsolved, but conspiracy theories abound. Some say Smalls had Shakur killed. One theory states that Knight killed Smalls out of revenge for Smalls killing Shakur. In other conspiracy theories, gangs, the police, and the FBI are blamed.

KEY PLAYERS

- Tupac Shakur was considered the face of West Coast rap before he was mysteriously murdered.

- Biggie Smalls was Shakur's East Coast counterpart, first his friend and then his rival. He was also mysteriously murdered.

- Suge Knight, cofounder of Death Row Records, was with Shakur when he was shot. Many people have suspected him in the murders of both Shakur and Smalls.

- Sean Combs, rapper and producer, is the head of Bad Boy Records. Combs, who worked closely with Smalls, was with Smalls the night he was murdered. Some people blame Combs for the death of Shakur.

- Orlando Anderson is the Crips gang member who several people claim shot Shakur after Anderson fought with Shakur and other members of the Death Row entourage.

IMPACT ON SOCIETY

Tupac Shakur and Biggie Smalls both had a huge impact on the music world. The artists rapped about the problems of urban poverty and violence. Shakur's work also covered racial injustice. Their deaths showed the damaging impact that a celebrity rivalry whipped up by media could have on individual people and on society. With their murders still officially unsolved, their legacies include the many conspiracy theories people have developed over the years. Fans also continue to enjoy music from both artists, years after their deaths.

QUOTES

"Because I'm talking about it doesn't mean that it's O.K."

—rapper Tupac Shakur, speaking to fans about the violence described in his music

"In street life, you're not allowed to show if you care about something. You've got to keep that straight face. The flip side of that is this album. He's giving up all his vulnerability."

—producer Sean "Diddy" Combs speaking in 1994 about Biggie Smalls's debut album
Ready to Die

GLOSSARY

affiliated
Officially attached or connected to an organization or group.

alleged
Accused without proof.

bail
A fee paid by an accused person so he or she can be released from jail until the case has concluded.

ballistics
The science of projectiles and firearms.

bond
A fee paid by someone else so that an accused person can be released from jail until the case has concluded.

coma
Unconsciousness due to disease, injury, or poison.

conspiracy theory
A belief, without proof, that someone is responsible for an event or crime.

dying declaration
A statement that someone makes when they know that they are dying.

entourage
A group of people who support or travel with someone else, usually an important person.

feud
An angry, long-lasting quarrel.

informant

A person who is not a police officer but works undercover for the police to get information.

magnet school

A type of public school that accepts students from a wide geographical area and usually has special programs or areas of study, such as science or performing arts.

medallion

A large piece of jewelry worn around the neck on a chain.

music manager

A person who guides the career of a musician.

platinum

An album is certified platinum when it sells a million units.

probation

The release of a prisoner who remains under supervision instead of incarceration.

production company

A business that produces films or music.

roadie

Someone who hauls and sets up equipment for a band or performer.

sting

An undercover law enforcement operation that, if successful, results in an arrest or citation for illegal activity.

ADDITIONAL RESOURCES

SELECTED BIBLIOGRAPHY

Baker, Soren. *The History of Gangster Rap*. Abrams, 2018.

Trend, David. *Everyday Culture: Finding and Making Meaning in a Changing World*. Paradigm, 2015.

Westhoff, Ben. *Original Gangstas*. Hachette, 2016.

FURTHER READINGS

Cummings, Judy Dodge. *Hip-Hop Culture*. Abdo, 2018.

Lusted, Marcia Amidon. *Hip-Hop Music*. Abdo, 2018.

ONLINE RESOURCES

Booklinks
NONFICTION NETWORK
FREE! ONLINE NONFICTION RESOURCES

To learn more about the murders of Tupac and Biggie, please visit **abdobooklinks.com** or scan this QR code. These links are routinely monitored and updated to provide the most current information available.

MORE INFORMATION

For more information on this subject, contact or visit the following organizations:

THE NATIONAL MUSEUM OF AFRICAN AMERICAN HISTORY AND CULTURE

1400 Constitution Ave. NW
Washington, DC 20560
844-750-3012
nmaahc.si.edu

The National Museum of African American History and Culture has multiple exhibits that feature hip-hop music and its impact on American culture.

THE NATIONAL MUSEUM OF AMERICAN HISTORY

1300 Constitution Ave. NW
Washington, DC 20560
202-633-1000
americanhistory.si.edu/exhibitions/places-invention

The National Museum of American History's Places of Invention exhibit features information on hip-hop music in the Bronx, New York, in the 1970s.

THE ROCK & ROLL HALL OF FAME

1100 Rock and Roll Blvd.
Cleveland, OH 44114
216-781-7625
rockhall.com

The Rock & Roll Hall of Fame's website includes information on inductees, including the artists they influenced and recordings of their songs. The museum has a Rapper's Delight exhibit and hosts live music events.

SOURCE NOTES

CHAPTER 1. SHOT IN VEGAS

1. Nick Bond. "On This Day: Mike Tyson Knocks Out Bruce Seldon with 'Phantom Punch.'" *Boxing News*, 7 Sept. 2018, boxingnewsonline.net. Accessed 15 Mar. 2019.

2. Natalie Finn. "The Unsolved Murder of Tupac Shakur: Untangling the Epic Layers of Mystery Surrounding the Case." *E! News*, 7 Sept. 2018, eonline.com. Accessed 15 Mar. 2019.

3. Finn, "The Unsolved Murder of Tupac Shakur."

4. Finn, "The Unsolved Murder of Tupac Shakur."

5. Ralph Bristout. "The Seven Day Theory: A Timeline of Tupac Shakur's Final Days." *Revolt TV*, 7 Sept. 2017, revolt.tv. Accessed 15 Mar. 2019.

6. James C. Howell and John P. Moore. "History of Street Gangs in the United States." *National Gang Center Bulletin*, May 2010, nationalgangcenter.gov. Accessed 6 Aug. 2019.

7. Bristout, "The Seven Day Theory."

8. Chuck Philips and Alan Abrahamson. "Police, Shakur's Entourage at Odds over Investigation." *Los Angeles Times*, 4 Feb. 1997, latimes.com. Accessed 15 Mar. 2019.

9. Philips and Abrahamson, "Police, Shakur's Entourage at Odds over Investigation."

10. Chuck Philips. "How Vegas Police Probe Floundered in Tupac Shakur Case." *Los Angeles Times*, 7 Sept. 2002, latimes.com. Accessed 15 Mar. 2019.

CHAPTER 2. TUPAC SHAKUR

1. "Tupac Shakur." *Biography*, 9 Jan. 2019, biography.com. Accessed 13 Mar. 2019.

2. George James. "Rapper Faces Prison Term for Sex Abuse." *New York Times*, 8 Feb. 1995, nytimes.com. Accessed 5 Apr. 2019.

3. "Tupac Shakur."

CHAPTER 3. BIGGIE SMALLS

1. Raekha Prasad. "My Boy Biggie." *Guardian*, 6 Dec. 1999, theguardian.com. Accessed 25 Mar. 2019.

2. Prasad, "My Boy Biggie."

3. Jayson Rodriguez. "Busta Rhymes Recalls Battling Jay-Z in High School." *MTV News*, 7 Oct. 2010, mtv.com. Accessed 6 Aug. 2019.

4. Prasad, "My Boy Biggie."

5. "Biggie Smalls." *Biography*, 15 Jan. 2019, biography.com. Accessed 14 Mar. 2019.

6. Touré. "Pop Music; Biggie Smalls, Rap's Man of the Moment." *New York Times*, 18 Dec. 1994, nytimes.com. Accessed 6 Aug. 2019.

7. Allison Cacich. "The Notorious B.I.G.'s Son C. J. Wallace Honors His Late Dad at the 2017 Billboard Awards." *Life and Style Magazine*. 21 May 2017, lifeandstylemag.com. Accessed 6 Aug. 2019.

CHAPTER 4. FRIENDS AND ENEMIES

1. Danilo Castro. "Biggie Smalls and 2Pac: 5 Fast Facts You Need to Know." *Heavy*. 19 Sept. 2017, heavy.com. Accessed 14 Mar. 2019.

2. Castro, "Biggie Smalls and 2Pac."

3. "Tupac Shakur." *Biography*, 9 Jan. 2019, biography.com. Accessed 13 Mar. 2019.

4. The Notorious B.I.G. "Who Shot Ya?" *Born Again*, Bad Boy Records, 1999.

5. Mike Destefano. "Eminem on the Significance of 2Pac's Biggie Diss Song 'Hit 'Em Up.'" *Complex*, 26 Dec. 2018, complex.com. Accessed 27 Mar. 2019.

6. Castro, "Biggie Smalls and 2Pac."

7. Soren Baker. *The History of Gangster Rap*. Abrams, 2018. 176.

CHAPTER 5. FROM SHAKUR'S DEATH TO SMALLS'S DEATH

1. Shaheem Reid. "Faith Evans Said Biggie Cried When He Heard Tupac Was Shot." *MTV*, 10 Sept. 2002, mtv.com. Accessed 29 Mar. 2019.

2. Reid, "Faith Evans Said Biggie Cried."

3. Chuck Philips. "Who Killed Tupac Shakur?" *Los Angeles Times*, 6 Sept. 2002, latimes.com. Accessed 29 Mar. 2019.

4. Reid, "Faith Evans Said Biggie Cried."

5. "Examining Similarities Between Biggie, Tupac Tragedies." *MTV*, 11 Mar. 1997, mtv.com. Accessed 29 Mar. 2019.

6. Cherise Johnson. "Suge Knight Hated Snoop Dogg for Squashing Beef with Biggie and Diddy." *Hip Hop DX*, 24 Aug. 2016, hiphopdx.com. Accessed 29 Mar. 2019.

7. Johnson, "Suge Knight Hated Snoop Dogg."

8. Ben Westhoff. *Original Gangstas*. Hachette, 2016. 354.

9. KlassicThrowbackTV. "Notorious B.I.G.'s Last TV Appearance (March 8th, 1997)." *YouTube*, 8 Mar. 2015, youtube.com. Accessed 19 Aug. 2019.

10. Shah Be Allah. "Today in Hip Hop History: Tupac Shakur's Fourth LP 'All Eyez On Me' Dropped 23 Years Ago." *Source*, 13 Feb. 2019, thesource.com. Accessed 29 Mar. 2019.

11. Westhoff, *Original Gangstas*, 355.

12. Westhoff, *Original Gangstas*, 355.

13. Erika Ramirez. "Biggie's Biggest: The Notorious B.I.G.'s Top 15 Billboard Hot 100 Hits." *Billboard*, 9 Mar. 2018, billboard.com. Accessed 6 Aug. 2019.

SOURCE NOTES CONTINUED

CHAPTER 6. THE INVESTIGATIONS

1. Sarah Ryley, Jeremy Singer-Vine, and Sean Campbell. "Shoot Someone in a Major US City, and Odds Are You'll Get Away with It." *BuzzFeed News*, 24 Jan. 2019, buzzfeednews.com. Accessed 17 June 2019.

2. "Biggie Smalls Wrongful Death Lawsuit Is Dismissed." *Variety*, 21 Apr. 2010, variety.com. Accessed 29 Mar. 2019.

3. Matt Miller. "Police Have Found the Gun That Killed Tupac." *Esquire*, 16 Dec. 2017, esquire.com. Accessed 30 Mar. 2019.

4. Justin Rohrlich and Don Sikorski. "Former FBI Agent: How the LAPD Derailed My Investigation into Biggie Smalls' Murder." *Daily Beast*, 10 Nov. 2018, thedailybeast.com. Accessed 30 Mar. 2019.

CHAPTER 7. GANG VIOLENCE

1. Jordan Runtagh. "The Truth behind Tupac Shakur's 1996 Murder: 'It was Simple Retaliation,' Reveals an LAPD Source." *People*, 13 Sept. 2017, people.com. Accessed 2 Apr. 2019.

2. Kyle Buchanan. "With One Strong Word, 'The Hate U Give' Couldn't Hold Its Tongue." *New York Times*, 18 Oct. 2018, nytimes.com. Accessed 6 Aug. 2019.

3. Ben Westhoff. *Original Gangstas*. Hachette, 2016. 296–297.

4. Nathan Rabin. "Everyone Knows Tupac the Rapper Was Great. What about Tupac the Actor?" *Vanity Fair*, 2 June 2017, vanityfair.com. Accessed 17 Mar. 2019.

5. Runtagh, "The Truth behind Tupac Shakur's 1996 Murder."

6. Jon Pareles. "Tupac Shakur, 25, Rap Performer Who Personified Violence Dies." *New York Times*, 14 Sept. 1996, nytimes.com. Accessed 2 Apr. 2019.

7. Paul Sacca. "Tupac's Murder Suspect Orlando Anderson Was Outed to Police by His Own Aunt According to Former LAPD Detective." *Bro Bible*, 24 Feb. 2019, brobible.com. Accessed 17 Mar. 2019.

8. Sacca, "Tupac's Murder Suspect Orlando Anderson Was Outed to Police by His Own Aunt According to Former LAPD Detective."

CHAPTER 8. SUGE KNIGHT

1. Joshua Espinoza. "Suge Knight's Ex-Wife: No Way in Hell I Would've Murdered Tupac." *Complex*, 5 Apr. 2017, complex.com. Accessed 3 Apr. 2019.

2. "Suge Knight's Ex-Wife Blasts Claims She Killed Tupac." *Page Six*, 5 Apr. 2017, pagesix.com. Accessed 3 Apr. 2019.

3. Emma Foster, "Suge Knight's Ex Wife Blasts Claims She Killed Tupac as 'Stupid Lies'—As Rap Mogul's Lawyer Denies Ever Making Claims." *Sun*, 5 Apr. 2017, thesun.co.uk. Accessed 6 Aug. 2019.

4. Connie Bruck. "The Takedown of Tupac." *New Yorker*. 7 July 1997, newyorker.com. Accessed 3 Apr. 2019.

5. Bruck, "The Takedown of Tupac."

6. Ted Rowlands and Michael Cary. "An AC 360° Cold Case: Mystery Still Surrounds Rappers' Deaths." *Anderson Cooper 360°*, 6 Jan. 2011, ac360.blogs.cnn.com. Accessed 6 Aug. 2019.

7. Bruck, "The Takedown of Tupac."

8. Bruck, "The Takedown of Tupac."

9. Richard Winton. "The Law Finally Catches Up with Suge Knight: A Timeline." *Los Angeles Times*, 20 Sept. 2018, latimes.com. Accessed 3 Apr. 2018.

10. Paul Sacca. "Tupac's Murder Suspect Orlando Anderson Was Outed to Police by His Own Aunt According to Former LAPD Detective." *Bro Bible*, 24 Feb. 2019, brobible.com. Accessed 17 Mar. 2019.

CHAPTER 9. SEAN "DIDDY" COMBS

1. Nick Reilly. "P. Diddy Responds to Eminem's Claim That He Killed Tupac." *NME*, 24 Sept. 2018, nme.com. Accessed 4 Apr. 2019.

2. Dory Jackson. "Eminem's Machine Gun Kelly Diss Track Randomly Name Drops Diddy and Tupac." *Newsweek*, 14 Sept. 2018, newsweek.com. Accessed 4 Apr. 2019.

3. Nick Reilly. "Jay Electronica Hits Out at Eminem over Lyric That Connected Diddy to Tupac's Death." *NME*, 17 Sept. 2018, nme.com. Accessed 9 Apr. 2019.

4. Reilly, "P. Diddy Responds to Eminem's Claim that He Killed Tupac."

5. "Eminem Accused for Accusing Diddy of Having Tupac Murdered on 'Killshot' Diss." *Capital Xtra*, 15 Sept. 2018, capitalxtra.com. Accessed 9 Apr. 2019.

6. Frannie Kelley. "'Can't Stop: Won't Stop': Bad Boy Records Was a Generation's Sound Track." *National Public Radio*, 22 June 2017, npr.org. Accessed 9 Apr. 2019.

7. Kelley, "'Can't Stop: Won't Stop.'"

8. Jesse Washington. "The Murder of Tupac Shakur Is a Tragedy—But the Why Is Not a Complete Mystery." *Undefeated*, 16 June 2017, theundefeated.com. Accessed 4 Apr. 2019.

9. "Puffy Tells MTV 'We Never Hired Crips.'" *MTV*, 25 Mar. 1997, mtv.com. Accessed 15 June 2019.

10. "Ex Bodyguard Eugene Deal Blames Diddy for Biggie's Murder." *Eurweb*, 23 July 2016, eurweb.com. Accessed 9 Apr. 2019.

11. Alistair McGeorge. "Sean 'Diddy' Combs Remembers Biggie Smalls with Touching Tribute 20 Years after His Death." *Mirror*, 9 Mar. 2017, mirror.co.uk. Accessed 14 June 2019.

CHAPTER 10. MORE CONSPIRACY THEORIES

1. "Is Tupac Alive? Suge Knight Says You Never Know." *BBC Newsbeat*, 22 Sept. 2017, bbc.co.uk. Accessed 30 Mar. 2019.

INDEX

ABOUT THE AUTHOR

Sue Bradford Edwards is a Missouri nonfiction author who writes about culture and history, including matters of race. She is the author or coauthor of 16 other titles from Abdo Publishing, including *Hidden Human Computers*, *What Are Race and Racism?*, and *Black Lives Matter*.